B
WES

Westfall, Patricia
    Tichenor.

Real farm

$14.95

DATE			
DEC 4 '93			

REAL·FARM

REAL·FARM

ENCOUNTERS WITH PERCEPTION

BY PATRICIA TICHENOR WESTFALL

NEW CHAPTER PRESS
NEW YORK

Library of Congress Catalog Card Number: 88-064093
ISBN: 0-942257-17-0

Editor: Ann Landi
Copy Editor: Brigid Mast
Jacket and Book Design: Christopher Lione
Illustrations: Brian Cronin

10 9 8 7 6 5 4 3 2 1

Manufactured in the United States of America

Portions of this book were previously published in *Country Journal*, *Esquire*,
and *Savvy* magazines.

This is a work of nonfiction; however, the name of my former husband
has been changed out of respect for his privacy.

To the memory of my father,
Harry F. Tichenor
1917–1975

CONTENTS

THE RED WHEELBARROW

CHAPTER ONE

THE RED WHEELBARROW

I used to ask friends to call me Patricia. I thought Patricia had a pretty sound, unlike Pat, which seemed abrupt, or Patty, which sounded too silly and girlish for a woman nearly six feet tall. Of course I asked Mark, shortly after we met, to call me Patricia, but to my surprise he refused, arguing that names are external—something parents or friends choose for us. Attempting to control my name might block love, he said: Names are doorways we carve to one another. Those were not his words, I'm sure—he always spoke in a rapid avalanche of metaphor that I find impossible to capture or mimic—but those were the ideas. Over the years he called me many names, even the dreaded Patty. In fact, especially in the word Patty were many doors.

We met on a picnic, a company picnic, of all things. I had just returned to the company, a publisher in Tennessee, after a dark six months away sorting out my life. Mark had joined the company in my absence as a gatherer-of-facts-by-phone. The job was temporary, something to see him through until a teaching job started up. The phone work bored him and put him in a foul mood most of the time, including at this picnic. The company bosses were in their hippie phase then, so the picnic was meant to be a consciousness-raising retreat. Before we got our chicken and potato salad, each of us had to give a short speech describing the most important thing in our lives.

I said the most important thing in my life was to get my four-hundred-pound couch out of the kitchen of my new apartment, where the carpet layers had left it. Mark said the most important thing in his life was poetry, and his greatest influence had been a poet with Wedgwood blue eyes.

Later I saw him standing by a tree and thought he looked more serious than a picnic required. He was too thin for his clothes, with arms longer than his sleeves. This gave him a preoccupied appearance, as if he had too much to think about for one lifetime. He was blond and had eyes, if not Wedgwood blue, then certainly intensely blue. I was sitting on a rock and asked if he'd like to share my rock. Someone took a picture of us on that rock and later gave it to us as a wedding present. It's the only photograph of him I've kept.

On that rock we had a magical conversation that started when he challenged something I was saying. I can't imagine what I said now, but it was probably an all-things-are-relative sort of comment. He said no, retorting with a quote from Blake that truth cannot be perceived and not be believed. I said perception could never be that objective. There were too many approaches to perception to know which approach to apply to truth. He didn't follow, so I offered to draw him a map of perception. I said it was also a map of the universe. My map was like this:

MEANING. . . . . LYRIC

A poetry professor of mine once had argued that all writing could be placed on an axis with meaning and lyric the extremes. The more lyrical a piece of writing, the more it resembled pure poetry, and the more absurd it was to read it for message or meaning. Meaning was prose.

I had liked that axis. I thought it described reality as well as poetry. The more spontaneous and spirited an event, the more absurd it was to explain it. Why explain the appeal of a tune? It was lyrical. On the other hand, why expect *joie de vivre* in a news report? It was meaning.

Mark still disagreed. He did not think meaning and lyric were opposite equals. As he argued, I placed dots on the line, writing the names of people next to them. I put one with my name slightly to the lyrical side of center and handed him the pencil. "Where do you put yourself?" I said.

Mark became strangely agitated. "It doesn't. . .this can't. I. . .I'm . . .here." He placed a dot off the line, above and beyond the lyric.

He studied the dot a minute, then nodded, satisfied with it. "Yes. Here."

Many, many times I had played this game and never before had anyone violated my axis. Not questioning my universe, people would place themselves on the line. Not Mark. My axis didn't hold him. He smiled, reading my surprise, and offered to help me move my couch. "Sunday," I said.

Sunday he arrived with a bottle of wine and a book of prose poems by W.S. Merwin. The wine was too dry and the book incomprehensible. I served a salad with celery and a casserole with eggplant. Celery and eggplant happened to be the only two vegetables in the universe Mark hated. We moved the couch in a sputter of polite but poor teamwork. And we talked. He did live in a world of poetry. Two poems from that awkward evening I especially remember. One was James Wright's "A Blessing," which ends

> Suddenly I realize
> That if I stepped out of my body I
> would break
> Into blossom

The other was William Carlos Williams's "The Red Wheelbarrow":

> so much depends
> upon
>
> a red wheel
> barrow
>
> glazed with rain
> water
>
> beside the white
> chickens

We were married the following Thanksgiving, which that year happened to be William Blake's birthday. For Mark's birthday the following year I gave him a red wheelbarrow. The chickens would follow four years after that when we bought a small farm in Iowa.

We moved to Iowa from Tennessee so Mark could work for a Ph.D. in English at the University of Iowa. Mark imagined this Iowa venture with the same intensity he had shown on the rock. My way of getting there would have been to go and see what was there. Show up—find a house. I'm not sure if that would have been lyrical or meaningful, but that's what I would have done. Mark, however, wrote fifty letters to Iowa City trying to find a house to rent.

It didn't work. Only a handful of the letters were answered and all said the same thing: It was hopeless. No rental housing was available in Iowa City. Hundreds of students were camping in tents waiting for freshmen with dorm space to get homesick or flunk out, the letters told us. A newspaper editor wrote telling of a woman who after a year and a half in the area was still living in her camper. So we wound up doing what I assumed all along we would do. That is, we packed up the car, the cat, and an eighteen-foot rental truck and drove to Iowa.

Then we parked the car, the cat, and the eighteen-foot rental truck at a motel and began looking. There were, of course, no houses for rent. There were, in fact, no apartments either. When we returned to renew our motel room for another night, we were also told there was no motel space that night because all rooms had been rented out months in advance to accommodate some golf tournament. We went finally to a rental agency and sat in a room full of desperate people, all waiting to pay twenty dollars to see a set of useless listings. "What do you think?" I said. "Should we leave and go see if the paper is out yet?"

"No," Mark said. "Let's try this first." We paid our twenty dollars, looked at their useless listings, and left—frightened. The rental truck had to be back in the morning or we'd have to begin paying a stiff daily rate. In the paper was one new listing: "eight-room farm-house." I sprang for a phone.

"Wait," said former New Yorker Mark. "How many real rooms is eight rooms?"

I said that if they counted the bathroom and pantry twice that was still more rooms than we'd had in Tennessee. We were the first to call and the first to see what to Ann, the landlady, was a private joy—the house she and her husband planned to live in when they retired from farming. It had a curved walnut banister, ornamental lead glass in the living room, floor-to-ceiling windows that actually opened, polished wood floors, ornate brass doorknobs, wallpaper and gables, a kitchen full of eastern light, and gingerbread trim outside. The house predated Iowa statehood, Ann told us.

Mark had become very silent as we walked through this marvel. "Patty," he whispered, "can we fill this?"

"We'll have to buy some furniture," I said.

"No," he said. "Can *we* fill it?"

I thought about his question for a few seconds. "I think so," I said.

There is no interesting way to describe what followed: Numbingly dull contentment. Mark was delighted with the university program and his teaching. I managed to work long distance for my former employer and also landed some part-time teaching in the university's journalism department. We lived in Ann's house for two years before buying our own farm. Ann, in fact, became a special friend. She took us for a wildflower walk in the woods behind their farm, and afterward, as we relaxed on her porch, she asked Mark, "Well, did you fill the house?"

Mark looked at her; it had been some months since we'd moved in. "We bought some furniture," he said cautiously.

"No," she said. "Did *you* fill it?"

Mark smiled. "I think so," he said.

We first saw the farm we were to buy when we were dinner guests of the owner, one of Mark's professors. My only memory of that evening is of snow piled outside the door and of some brass coat hooks by the kitchen door. Around that time Mark had been writing a poem I liked about owls, which had recently begun perching on our roof at night. He wrote about how in the stillness that follows making love one discovers the stillness of night, and the haunting soft stillness of the owls' intimate whooing above us. Just from curiosity, Mark checked the library to learn the symbolism of owls and came home upset to have found that in several folklores the owl was a symbol of death.

Mark's professor died that December.

His widow decided to sell almost immediately, so we offered to look. We spent a long afternoon tramping through woods and snow, seeing what twenty acres can be. The land was steep, too hilly for crops and had an erosion problem. The woods were overgrazed, so most of the trees were under stress. The house was cozy, but small. The barn roof had buckled and its foundation was crumbling. The shed leaked. The garage was on the verge of collapse. But there was a working windmill; it actually pumped the farm's water. It was the windmill that won us. We bought the farm for that windmill.

THE WINDMILL

CHAPTER TWO

THE WINDMILL

When I was a girl, windmills were about the only relief from cornfields during interminable drives between Chicago and my downstate aunts. We children never knew what windmills did for farmers, but they served us nicely. We competed to see whose side of the car had more—extra points for spotting one spinning. I still feel extra-points pleased when I see one in motion. But until we owned a windmill in Iowa I hadn't noticed they were disappearing.

As windmills go, ours was average, standing only two-and-a-half stories high on its tapering metal tower. Like the ones I had passed as a kid, it was the most imposing feature on the farm. It demanded viewing. The shape of the buildings, color of the roofs, number of trees below—none of this was visible when the windmill was spinning. More than once I'd sit in the east pasture just to watch it spin.

I always thought the wheel, with its petal-like sails, was the essence of windmill reality. But once I began depending on one for water, I saw that a thin shaft of cedar dropping from a gearbox on top to a steel pumping rod at ground level was the heart of the machine. This shaft rose and fell once with every full spin of the wheel. On the upstroke roughly a gallon of water splashed into a two-thousand-gallon cistern buried near the house. On a good windy day the windmill would fill the cistern.

We began noticing windmill shafts shortly after we bought the farm, and saw with growing worry that not one of the twenty or so windmills standing by roads we frequented had shafts intact. Most of these windmills stood motionless. A few had gears permanently engaged and spun all the time. But ours was the only one—for miles—that actually pumped a well. Why?

The widow who sold us the farm had shown us how to turn it on by lifting a lever to engage the gears. She also taught us to adjust valves in the well to shunt water away from the house to the barn or hog shed. We would learn very soon that there was more to windmills than levers and valves.

Our first few weeks on the farm were rough ones; at least we two urban products thought so. Our past had not prepared us for the troubles we were finding. Mark would come in almost daily and announce that he'd found a rapidly eroding gully, a crack in a foundation, rot in some wood, algae in the pond, a diseased tree, a patch of ground going to seed in weeds so vigorous they were decreed by Iowa law to be "legally noxious." I dismissed such worries. I may have been from Chicago, but he was from New York, so he was the genuine city kid here. What did he know of country trauma? One morning, though, I announced bad news, which meant for once we had a problem. The wind was brisk that morning, yet when I engaged the gears, the windmill did not spin. We'd had a severe thunderstorm the night before.

"I'll call the insurance company," Mark said.

"Windmill? What windmill?" the insurance man asked. "Obviously, we can't insure windmills," he gently added.

Obviously? What was so awful about windmills? With that "obviously" sitting ominously in our minds, we next proceeded to stand on the ground looking up. This produced no useful information. Next we went to an upstairs window and scanned the mechanism with binoculars, but the gears were encased in a cone-shaped box; there was no seeing trouble even if we had known how trouble might look. Then we noticed a construction of sorts on the south side of the scaffold, a ladder apparently, but one with steps so narrow hands could not be placed side by side on a rung.

Mark stared at that ladder.

Mark went outside and walked toward that ladder. He and I had once hiked to a fire tower in the Tennessee Smokies and decided to climb it for the view. It had civilized stairs, but I stopped at the third platform, too dizzy and nauseated to climb higher. Mark made it to the top and back but only by carefully, cautiously feeling his way, holding with both hands to the rails, stopping many times to clear his dizziness. When we both reached the ground again, we sat breathing hard, trying to calm ourselves. While we rested, another couple arrived at the tower, ran up the stairs, and leaned over the rails. They even ate their lunch up there. We slunk away, two embarrassed acrophobes.

Mark and I differed in our fears. He was afraid to look up; I can't look down. Once while hiking in the Colorado Rockies, we stranded ourselves on a ledge. The only way to escape was to climb up and sideways toward a flatter area. We made it only because he coaxed me over the spots where we had to look down and I coaxed him when we had to look up. We never went to the mountains again.

Mark climbed three sections of the windmill tower—about fifteen feet—and stopped, obviously dizzy. "I can't," he said and came slowly back down. Pushed by some odd impulse, I then walked over and relifted the gear lever. Immediately the vane swung around and the wheel began spinning. We stood there stupefied until Mark noticed the wind had changed direction.

Yes, of course, we were glad nothing was wrong, but, yes, we felt stupid not to have realized that with windmills, wind mattered. We decided we needed to talk to somebody who knew windmills. That, we were told, would be Robert Wieland of Riverside.

We telephoned him. He appeared as requested. No, actually he exploded upon us. He screeched into our barnyard and crashed into a ditch. "Don't you folks mow?" he bellowed from the cab. Out he burst, a not-tall, not-short, not-stocky, not-slight construction of energy with white, ramrod-straight hair, coveralls, and a voice that never ceased. He allowed us no moment for defense or apology, but ran to open the truck's camper doors, hauled out two boards, commanded us to position them thus and so, pried his truck up and backed it out—*bim, bam*—in command and talking all the while.

When the truck was safely out of the ditch, Mark turned to me and asked if I had the list of questions ready. He turned back, the homeowner prepared to direct the serviceman to his bidding, but Wieland was gone. We heard him, of course.

"Well, what's the trouble?" he hollered from the top of the windmill.

"The trouble's down here," Mark said. He was smiling slightly, anticipating a tussle of wills.

"Oh, what trouble is that?" Wieland said. He had the Iowa habit of preceding most sentences with "well" or "oh" or "oh, well."

"We can't get water to the outbuildings," Mark said.

"Oh, I'm not a wellman," Wieland announced firmly. He was climbing back down. "I don't do wells." He was on the ground and lifting the boards off the well head. "Not wells."

"You a specialist?" Mark asked.

He laughed. "That's right. A specialist. You want your well fixed, you call a wellman." He was now sitting on the well stones. "What's wrong with it?"

"I thought you didn't do wells," Mark said.

"Well, I know a thing or two. What's wrong?"

"Can't get water out to the barn," Mark said.

Wieland ordered Mark down into the well, and under his coaching, Mark had the pump apart in a minute. "Oh, there's your trouble; your leathers are worn. You get a wellman to put in some new ones." For a man who didn't do wells he proceeded to tell us more about wells than did the wellman who came a few days later and spoke to us in an argot we couldn't begin to comprehend.

"Well, let's look at this windmill," Wieland said when Mark had reassembled the pump, and back up the tower he scampered. Will tussling was over. Wieland might do as he pleased, and mostly he pleased to talk. "Well, here now, this shaft looks good; been replaced recently; well, the gears look okay; well, here. . ." Abruptly the tenor of his voice changed ever so slightly. "Well, here, young fella, why don't you come up here?"

There was no mistaking Wieland's tone. He had hurled a challenge. Immediately he tried to soften it. "You come up here and I'll show you how to change the oil. Well, go on. There's another hard hat and safety belt in the truck."

Mark stood for a second. I expected him to laugh his no thanks because he was usually immune to this game, especially in Iowa. Maybe if we were in New York he'd think about such a ploy—I can't say. But here in Iowa he easily resisted the posturings, the Iowa delight in big, big machines, for example, or the Iowa fascination with injuries. This was all meaningless macho to someone with roots in New York City. But Mark surprised me; this dare he took. He walked to the truck, got the safety gear, and climbed the windmill.

He would say later he did it for the chance to learn from Wieland. But I suspected his real reason was he couldn't allow a sassy white-haired Iowan to taunt him from the top of his own windmill. Mark climbed slowly, but he climbed, and I watched him perch beside Wieland to rock on the balls of his feet because the platform at the top was too small for a whole foot.

To complete the ritual Wieland, of course, acted as if people joined him at the tops of windmills every day. But later, when it was time to swap stories, he delighted us with tales of other people's fear of heights.

While I paced below, Mark and Wieland chatted above. He told Mark our windmill was the "latest model," a 1935 Aermotor. He knew that because it had a tail spring to prevent it from spinning too fast and breaking a rod in high winds. I couldn't hear all they were saying; their voices dipped as they became more intent on the machine. In a while Mark began backing down the ladder, holding a can with the spent oil in one hand.

"How old do you think he is?" Mark whispered when he reached me.

"Maybe fifty-five, maybe sixty," I said.

"He's seventy-four."

I couldn't believe it; nothing about that man was old. But he said he remembered when the Aermotor Company made its last major design change, encasing the gears in a cone. "That was 1915, and it was a big improvement too, let me tell you. In the box, the gears are bathed in oil all the time, so you only have to change the oil once every year or two. Before then you might have to oil it two or three times a month."

Boxing the gears was surprisingly good for the windmill-repair business. Before they were encased, it was too expensive for most families to hire someone so often. That meant the terror of climbing the tower fell to whoever in the family could stand it, or more likely, could least stand the awful screech the unoiled gears made. Since women were about the house more than men, they usually got tired of the racket soonest and did most of the windmill climbing. Somewhere in the Smithsonian is a placard that quotes a rural editor as saying a country woman really needed only two skills: firing a shotgun and climbing a windmill.

The gearbox changed all that. A once-a-year oil change was cheap enough that even the thriftiest families would rather call Wieland than climb themselves. At his peak, in the 1930s, Wieland serviced over a hundred and fifty wells in a six-county area.

Wieland didn't remember Aermotor's other big innovation: metal. But his grandfather had been a windmill man when metal became the norm. "My grandfather—he always would say 'damn my shirt' when he was mad. 'Damn my shirt,' just like that. He built wooden windmills back when they were built on the ground and had to be hoisted into place with a winch." In those days, building windmills was a highly skilled, expensive task. Few people could afford the luxury, but when the Aermotor Company started making them of metal in the 1860s, the business changed radically. After that anyone who could tighten a bolt could assemble a windmill. Aermotor sold thousands of kits by mail. Dozens of other windmill companies sprang into business, and their salesmen traveled door to door throughout rural America. By the turn of the century, an estimated six million windmills were in operation on U.S. farms. They brought an astonishing luxury to the farm—water. In a fifteen-mph wind, a twelve-foot wheel could pump an incredible thirty-five gallons per minute. To the farmer, there simply was no comparison between a windmill and the old oaken bucket.

These two innovations, metal parts and an enclosed gearbox, were the only things really different about the American windmill. The rest of the apparatus—radiating instead of vertical sail blades, a tail vane to keep the blades facing into the wind, a gear-and-cam assembly to move a shaft up and down—all this had been windmill reality around the world for decades or, in some instances, centuries. The use of metal made windmills a common item in America. The gearbox made them less bother.

After a time Wieland hollered at me to engage the gears. This didn't sound like a good idea. "It's awfully windy," I advised. Mark frowned down at me. He couldn't believe I was rude enough to argue with a seventy-four-year-old windmiller who'd been working the machines for more than half a century. "Turn it on," he snapped.

I did, but I spent the next few minutes frantic with worry, convinced a gust of wind would come up, sweep the tail vane around and knock them both to certain death. Wieland knew otherwise.

Wieland went into windmilling because it was safer than anything else he'd done. Although he'd worked around windmills since he was a teenager, they had been a part-time thing for him. His real business was farming. One day he'd been taking a cornpicker off a tractor when the machine came down on him, pinning his head and ripping out an eye. "My face was tore up so bad I couldn't swallow for six months, had no saliva. I lost the eye and my nose had to be repaired. My hair turned white, this white, over the next two days from the scare. My son says he never had anything more awful happen to him than the day he saw me bleeding like that. That's when I quit farming and went to this full time. Of course, you have to watch your business in this too."

The biggest hazard is not the wind, as I'd feared. "That's the only way you can see if the machine is working, if it's a little windy." The real danger is ice. "The only time I've been injured is in wintertime. I went up without my hard hat on and a couple of pieces of ice came down and cut my head. With Aermotors, if ice gets around the collar up there it won't go, and someone has to climb up there and chip all the ice off. I talked to one fellow, though, and he says what he does is take a shotgun out there and shoot off the ice."

Mark's eyes lit up when he heard this. His favorite fantasy was his imaginary machine gun mounted on the hood of the pickup. Shooting a windmill sounded like a fine idea to him. Me, I had to wreck the fantasy by wanting to know if that could hurt the windmill.

"This guy says it don't," Wieland said. "That's what he told me. I've never tried it though. Maybe if you try it, be careful not to shoot the sails." He turned this over in his mind a moment. "Yeah, don't shoot the sails."

Wieland said he now serviced no more than two dozen windmills, although some of these he'd been oiling since the 1920s. "There's a few working windmills and windmill repairmen in the Amish towns. They still use them, but they keep to themselves. Except for them, you could say I'm the last windmill repairman in Iowa, the last one in southeast Iowa, for sure."

But why were windmills and windmill repairmen disappearing? I told Wieland what we'd seen around us—windmills with no shafts, none pumping a well. After talking with him it seemed crazy that folks weren't using them. They were so simple. You remembered to turn them on and off every few days. You oiled them every couple of years. That was it. Maybe occasionally they iced up or broke a shaft or wore out a gear. These were easy repairs. A windmill made of galvanized metal could conceivably work for centuries. So why?

"Most folks use them now for television antennas," Wieland said. "Others for weather vanes. One guy called me, he wanted me to take the wheel off his and put a seal for a vane up there. His name was Seal, you see. And last fall this fellow from Mount Pleasant sold his farm but kept the windmill. He put up a fancy hundred-thousand-dollar house on his new farm and had me put up the windmill but with no well under it. When I was done he thought it was a trifle too high. It was forty feet. He had me take it down and cut it down to thirty-five feet, to show up the house a little nicer, he said."

"In part, that's wonderful, and, in part, that's silly," I said.

"Well, it is silly, and I asked him why go to all this trouble, and he just kept saying, 'The farm wouldn't look right without it.' "

Wieland had done that before, put up a windmill with no well under it, but most of the ones he worked had been up a long time. "The tallest one I work, it's seventy-five feet tall, stands right out in the open prairie. They told me it was tall because when it went up, there were tall trees there, but now it stands alone, outlasted the trees. They don't use it, but they keep it working because they said their dad would go crazy if they took it down. So they were keeping it working till he died. Then he did die, but they still keep it working."

"Do you think they'll ever come back, like use them for electricity?" I asked him.

"Well, no. People forget we did all that already. In the thirties and forties. 'Windchargers,' they called them. Aermotor sold them. Later Monitor came out with something. In those days, a man was lucky if he had a refrigerator and a lamp or two, yet they couldn't keep even that little bit running with a windmill. A man had to use his truck to charge his batteries."

"A windmill couldn't run your electric well?" I said.

"Well, no," he laughed.

"But they pump water so effortlessly," I said. "Why don't folks use them that way, the way they were meant?" I couldn't let the question go; I had to know what was "wrong" with windmills.

"Well, folks don't have big cisterns like you do. Maybe they don't have room to store more than twenty gallons, so if the wind doesn't blow, they don't have water, or they have to pump by hand."

That made sense. I couldn't see me filling a washing machine by hand pump. But later I got to thinking: The wind did blow.

Almost every day there was enough to pump some water. It was also easy to attach an electric motor to the pump rod for those rare days when it was truly calm. The widow had done that. We'd never used this motor except once to see if it worked. It seemed easier to us just to be careful—to not water the orchard on a calm day, for example. Storage didn't seem to me enough of a problem to abandon this perfect machine; no maintenance, no smell, no cost for energy, and best of all, no racket. The windmill had a delightful sound, something like a cross between a cricket's chirp and a heartbeat.

When the wellman came the next week, there was only one sentence we understood: his first. "This well is bad," he said. He had us grasp the pump rod as if that would make things clear to us. He gave the well six months until it failed. Naturally he was quite cheerful at the prospect, for drilling a well meant billing a customer; $3,600 was his rough estimate.

That night was the first sleepless one I'd ever known Mark to spend. If on top of the erosion, algae, diseased trees, collapsing outbuildings, if the well were to go. . . . Not to mention the money; where would we get the money? A friend saw us in town the next day and instead of greeting us with "hello," said, "What's wrong?" We were too gloomy to answer. "Your car," he said. Our car was notorious for its poor health.

"No, for once it's not the car," Mark said. "It's something worse."

The friend was puzzled. What on earth could be worse than a car on the fritz? He wrinkled his face, struggling to imagine something more dreadful. Finally he blurted, "Your refrigerator, it's your refrigerator."

I laughed, but the moment was troubling for its unwelcome clarity. I don't like seeing how far my generation has come from the basics. What could be more basic than water? Water would be the first thing our grandparents would have guessed. In the days thereafter we began to understand why abandoned windmills predominate. Windmills last forever. Wells don't.

At a neighbor's I had noticed six metal caps over old wells, but I'd never wondered why so many. Whenever a well fails, the windmill either has to be moved or left to rust, and wells used to fail frequently. Most folks like windmills. They like them so much that six-foot toy windmills are a popular lawn ornament in Iowa, perhaps second only to plastic deer. Yet when the hassle of moving a real one is set beside the convenience of installing an electric pump, convenience wins. Convenience has been winning for over a generation.

The six months passed. The windmill pumped faithfully. Its shadow flickered reassuringly across my back as I gardened, or disrupted the kitchen light as I drank my morning coffee. It creaked with stable steadiness month after month with no hint of trouble, but what had before been a hypnotic delight was now a source of quiet worry. I looked at it with a sense of impending loss. When the well failed, I thought, the windmill might have to be torn down. I didn't think I could endure that. The farm wouldn't look right without it.

REAL FARM

CHAPTER THREE

REAL FARM

The farm was to be a real farm. This Mark insisted upon constantly, particularly whenever I balked at some plan of his. If we were to live these twenty-three miles from town, we had to approach this fully committed, use the twenty acres to their fullest potential. This was not a house with a large yard. This was a farm.

To Mark, "real farm" meant installing a woodstove, building a greenhouse, buying a tractor, and establishing a cash crop of some sort. To me, "real farm" meant chickens.

When Mark announced to University of Iowa English Professor David Morrell that I wanted chickens, Professor Morrell told Mark that his experience with chickens was limited but his impression was that they were filthy and stupid. This Mark repeated to me.

When Mark told Departmental Administrator Felicia Lavallee that I wanted chickens, she told him she had a horror of chickens because they were filthy and stupid. This he repeated to me.

He told Associate Professor of Rhetoric Cleo Martin, who had raised chickens as a farm girl. She remembered them as filthy and stupid, a memory Mark repeated to me.

He told Rebecca Johnson, reference librarian. She told him she'd had a duck once who would eat anything yellow.

He told Assistant Professor of German Geoffrey Waite, who was visiting us. Geoff stared solemnly at his hands at this announcement and then said quietly, "Immanuel Kant says, 'If you would look in the eye of stupidity, look into the eye of a chicken.'"

Geoff Waite was a frequent visitor to the farm, one who knew he was privileged to arrive unexpectedly. I don't ever recall not being glad to see him, although one of his visits frightened my sister. She was staying with us for a few days and was alone in the house when Geoff marched in carrying a daisy he had found in the yard. He stood over her dropping petals one by one upon her hair. "This is it," she thought, "it" being horrors unspeakable, yet terrifyingly imaginable. She sat waiting tensely for "it," but Geoff went outside and climbed the windmill instead. He was perched contentedly up there when we arrived home. My sister was behind locked doors.

"It's all right, Mary. He's a friend of ours."

"Are you sure?"

Geoff never visited us without also going to see the chickens. And he never visited the chickens without saying to them, "Kant says, 'If you would look in the eye of stupidity. . . .'"

Pat wants chickens, Mark told Professor of English William Murray. "Then they must be special chickens," said Professor Murray, and he told us there was a hatchery in Webster City, Iowa, that sold attractive breeds, but he couldn't remember the name of it. We checked. The name Professor Murray couldn't remember was Murray McMurray Hatchery. I ordered ten Rhode Island Reds, ten White Rocks, and ten Barred (or black and white) Rocks. Rocks, I presumed, were chickens. I had decided I didn't want to depend on only white birds. I wanted visual delight, a kaleidoscope of feathers. "Real farm" meant seeing color from my study window.

To prepare for the chickens, I read. The more I read, the more I realized reading was a mistake. No one who wrote pamphlets was in any way close to my way of thinking. That anything could depend on any color wheelbarrow, with or without rainwater, was reality beyond these booklets. They aimed to maximize production. They assumed a minimum of three hundred to five hundred chicks plus timed lighting systems, cages, medicated feeds, specially designed buildings, and uniformly boring birds.

I was horrified. For example, a leading question in my mind was what to feed them. No pamphlet wrote about food. Instead they discussed "nutrient requirements," and either told me the obvious ("Peanut meal is used where peanuts are grown"), or mystified me by noting that cottonseed meal was low in methionine and lysine and contained gossypol. But what did chickens *eat*?

The pamphlets all talked about "culling the poor layer," and described, in what I'm sure they considered graphic detail, a method for examining a hen to determine whether or not it lay eggs (or, rather, "effected gallinaceous ovulation"). I knew these paragraphs were graphic; the word "moist" was my clue. But other than that word, I had no idea what the texts were saying.

Part of the problem, of course, was that I'd never seen a chicken anywhere except wrapped in grocery store polymers. I did read one good poultry book, a British text published in 1581. I spent several happy days poring over a microfiche of that book; it was the only one I understood, though some of its methods struck me as a few centuries out of date. So I gave up reading and decided to do my learning when I had live birds to learn from. If I could study gardening by observing the garden, surely I could learn about chickens the same way. Besides, chickens were probably better at communicating their needs than were asparagus.

Mark was uncomfortable with this strategy. Someone who could write fifty letters for something as trivial as an apartment hunt would expect total and absolute intensity for a genuinely important project like chickens. Never mind that the effort, like the fifty letters, was futile. Energy, no matter how pointless, was a virtue to him, and my decision to wait was definitely unvirtuous.

I had decided the chicks would live in the one-time hog house behind the garden, so I skipped over any prose about housing. Mark read these paragraphs, though, and began doubting whether the hog house was good enough. He kept underlining sentences about floor space, heating systems, watering systems, ramps, roosts, electronic doors. When he began drawing plans for a solar-heated poultry operation, I rebelled. We had too much else to do to put that kind of effort into thirty chickens. The hog house was fine, I said. It was big, sunny, and solid. I had once considered using it for a study. If it was good enough for me, it was more than good enough for chickens.

By then professors, administrators, and librarians had convinced Mark that chickens were filthy and stupid. So he decided this was now my project and I could be as unprepared as I pleased. The chicks arrived the first of May. The post office called that morning to tell me to be home at mail time. Mark went on to campus alone; I spent the morning fluttering. Finally, I organized myself and hauled four old doors I'd found in the basement to the hog house. I gathered some chicken wire and tools. Then I made a chick-sized waterer from a coffee can and a pie plate—a neighbor had taught me that trick. I stole the cold frame from the garden for a brooder—I'd thought of that myself just a few days before. I converted it by tacking blue jeans around the bottom and hanging a heat lamp over the glass. Lastly I swiped the thermometer from the refrigerator. My brooder was complete.

I felt pleased enough with myself after that to sprawl on the grass and enjoy this perfect May day, warm enough for lying in the sun in a long-sleeved shirt. When the mail carrier pulled into the driveway, he told me he'd had music all morning long. He needn't have said so; I couldn't believe how loudly they chirped.

He handed me the box. I set it on the cart and began trying to hurry to the hog house, now chicken house, but I was trembling. I laughed at myself: I was trembling, I was forgetting to breathe. I was nervous and felt foolish for being nervous. If mere chickens (and chickens were always "mere" to the neighbors) could affect me so, how would I ever handle a pig or ducks or geese or sheep or goats? I wanted all of these, especially the goats. Surely I would have to be less awestruck or I would never cope. Maybe Mark's approach was right; prior effort might be good emotional preparation even if it was a waste of practical time. I sat on the ground, figuring the chicks would live a few minutes more while I got myself under control.

I remembered from the books that chicks had to be taught to eat and drink. So I set food and water beside the brooder, surrounded it with a circle of cardboard, and sat inside this circle with the box of chirping chicks on my lap. I opened it. They cowered, abruptly silent at the sight of me. They were mixed together, red, yellow, and black, and were much larger than I had expected. One chick was noticeably different, with distinct stripes and bluish-green feet. I remembered the catalog promising to throw in an extra "rare chick" with each order. This must have been the rare bird. I reached in and they ran in a mass away from my hand. Not one peeped. For the moment we're equal, I thought. Neither of us has seen anything quite like the other before. I took one out, a red one, and gently bumped its head into the water dish. It understood immediately and began drinking, first taking a sip, then lifting its head to swallow. Its fear of me was gone. I repeated this at the food dish. Then I sat the chick under the heat lamp. It sat for a second, then peeped.

One by one I taught the birds to drink and eat. I noticed suddenly I was talking to them. You're talking to birds, I thought. One would not learn, and I set it aside until I finished with the others. Lastly I tried the reluctant chick again, bumping its head into the water over and over about a dozen times, until finally, stupid thing, it caught on.

By the time I finished, two or three of the chicks under the lamp were sprawled on their sides. Dead? I thought and poked them. No. Asleep. I watched them for a while. Some were exploring, some sleeping. Finally a few ventured out beyond the brooder's blue-jean curtain and found the food again. I went into the house, exhausted, and, like the chicks, I took a nap.

When Mark returned home that afternoon, I was back in the chicken house, hammering, trying to rig up a cat-, rat-, and varmint-proof enclosure around the brooder. About eight o'clock, after several trips out to generously critique my progress, Mark decided to yield and help me. By then I'd managed to piece the four doors together into an approximation of a box. The problem was how to make four oddly sized doors and a snatch of chicken wire into a structure that would keep critters out but let me in to feed them and let electrical cords out to heat them. It was a major engineering problem, complicated by my major lack of skill in driving a common nail. Mark found a fifth door somewhere, an old screen, and gathered some baling twine. The twine did it. That had been the missing essential. The box was complete.

"It's awful," Mark said.

"It's beautiful," I said.

He groused about the mismatched corners, the flaccid way the chicken wire undulated over the top, how the screen-door lid with baling-twine latch failed to either lid or latch. I marveled at how calm the chicks had been in the uproar, how they'd chirped and eaten, napped and played the entire time we'd been hammering. We fussed over these aesthetic matters all the way back into the house and into bed and were still fussing sleepily in the dark.

On one of his visits to the chicks to quote Kant to them, Geoff Waite observed to Mark that all of my chicks were roosters. Geoff and Mark hurried into the house to tell me this news. A neighbor was visiting, so all four of us ran back out to the chicken house. I said they couldn't all be roosters; it was a law of nature that half had to be hens. The neighbor, who had more expertise in these matters, looked the situation over gravely. He said they all looked like roosters to him.

"This could only happen to us," Mark said.

Several weeks later, Geoff was visiting again so out we went to quote and recount. They all still looked like roosters.

During their entire chickhood, the chicks endured repeated hammering. I finished building the fence around their scratching yard minutes before I decided they had to get outside or perish of rickets. I finished a wall and a door to separate their end of the chicken house from a storage area seconds before I felt I had to let them out of their box or watch them smother. In fact, I used one of the sides from their box as the door for their area. I finished the nesting box only a day before the first of those roosters laid an egg. Actually, I would have had the nesting box finished three days earlier, but it took me three attempts before I built one that wouldn't collapse. My carpentry skills were very raw in those days.

In the end, eleven of the original thirty-one turned out to be hens. By my count, that still defied the laws of nature. The rest really were roosters and so destined for the freezer, all except the chick with green feet. He was becoming stunningly beautiful. He had a rose comb; that is, the mass of flesh on his head resembled a flower, not an epiglottis. His feathers were silken and sweeping, of a silvery color with iridescent green spangles. His feathers would sway in a breeze if he perched on a fencepost, and he loved to perch as high as he could to show off his splendor. He wasn't much of a crower, but he was much too pretty to eat. Mark named him Sam.

I had marked on the calendar a day to "dress"—as the neighbors put it—our first chicken. I looked forward to this day not for the dressing part, but for the eating. Everyone told us how much better fresh-killed chicken tasted than store-bought. We imagined the contrast to be something like the difference between fresh and store-bought corn. Dressing day arrived, a Saturday. Mark and I fixed breakfast. Mark and I lingered over coffee. Mark and I eyed each other. "Let's go," Mark said. I had tried to read about dressing too, and I knew I didn't understand what to do. But. Onward.

Usually I'd let the chickens out before breakfast, but this morning I'd kept them penned in to make it easier to catch one. We selected one and began trying to corner it. He outmaneuvered us no matter which way we stepped, so we selected another, which outmaneuvered us no matter which way we stepped, so we selected another. After about half an hour of chasing chickens, Mark finally had one by the leg. He was hollering and cursing by then, and I'm afraid I was laughing, but at least he had one.

It flapped, shrieked, kicked, and pecked at him, but Mark held on. We took it outside to a stump, still flapping. Mark tried to hold it down while I raised the hatchet. I was afraid I might hit

Mark so I hit nothing, neither chicken nor Mark nor stump, though I did graze the grass slightly. In disgust, Mark took the hatchet from me and managed to separate the head from the neck, more by mashing than by axing. Had us a freshly killed chicken, we did. Now what?

I reasoned that feathers were next and began pulling them out, Mark helping, but the feathers were firmly part of the skin and we wound up removing most of the skin as well. Mark by then was quite sure he was needed in the woods. Muttering something about chickens being my project, he fueled up the chain saw and left. I proceeded into the kitchen to figure out how to convert this bruised object in the sink into something resembling the perfections at the store. When Mark returned from the woods he found me sitting in the kitchen rocker, my face an ashen shade of green.

"That bad?" he said.

It wasn't the butchery that bothered me, I said. It was the botching of it. It should have been graceful, quick. We give them trouble-free lives, and they give their lives to us, but part of the contract should be a quick, perfect death and dressing.

"Do you want to go out for dinner?" Mark said.

"No." I was determined to have fried chicken, fresh chicken, for dinner. I cooked the bird, and it was tough, almost inedible. I felt awful. Mark tried to cajole me into a better mood, but I was too disappointed. If only it had tasted good. The next morning, Ann, our former landlady, called. She asked if our chickens were old enough to dress and would we like a dressing lesson. She laughed when I told her about the disaster the day before, and she promised to be there a few days later.

As soon as Ann and her daughter, Tracy, arrived the following Wednesday, she told me to put a big pot on to boil. When the steam was just so—not boiling but close—she led us out to the chicken house. She bent down and picked up a chicken. Tracy did the same. She held its wings pinned against its legs so it couldn't flap, then whacked its head off briskly. The chicken hardly realized it was caught before it was dead. Tracy was just as quick.

She sank the bird into the water, neck end first, explaining that wing feathers needed more heat than legs. Then she dunked the leg end, counted for five seconds, and tested by rubbing the leg. "You don't want to cook the fat, just soften it. Now rub off the feathers; don't pull." By then I had taken Tracy's bird to try to get the feel of this myself.

She gutted and cleaned the bird swiftly. I followed along, less swiftly, less neatly, but with considerably more grace than the first time. These chickens were too young to be tough, she told me; maybe cooking it without the skin had made it tough. She was right. These second birds were wonderful, the meat sweet-tasting, moist, and tender.

Weeks later, when we'd dressed and frozen the last of the roosters, I told her I had mastered all she had taught me except one thing. I never did get the knack of simply bending down and seizing a chicken. I always had a ferocious chase before I caught one. She laughed and at Christmas gave me a long wire with a bend in one end—a chicken-catching wand, she explained.

I never lost my awe of the hens. They were businesslike creatures; every morning seven or eight of them would take turns hopping into the nesting box to lay their eggs. Every day. Some days I would have eleven eggs, never less than six. We'd been used to eating maybe seven or eight eggs a week, so it didn't take long for this miracle to become something of a problem. I discovered there are not many recipes that call for fifteen eggs, separated. I made quiches, fruitcakes, sponge cakes, and eggnogs, and finally had to sell three dozen eggs a week to professors, administrators, and librarians, or grow fat. I suppose I could have given the eggs away, but selling them made me feel more like a real farmer.

As I watched the hens I began to wonder why no one has yet described their real function. Every "organic-method" gardening book or article I've read mentions the importance of chickens for creating a "closed cycle" garden. That is, the garden is supposed to feed the chickens, and the chicken droppings are to feed the garden. But these pragmatic authors ignore the energy hens bring to their lives. They were always greatly animated. If one found a bug, all would run over to have a look, as if it were the most interesting bug ever. Any momentary variation, no matter how trivial, seemed exciting and important to them. If a hen took a dust bath, it was with total abandon, as if this was the first and last dust bath ever to be. If I tossed them wilted dinner scraps, even those from several dinners ago, this gift was greeted with such clacking and fluttering it seemed like joy to me. Overripe tomatoes, overlarge cucumbers, bolted lettuce—no matter what I gave them, they greeted it with more gratitude, enthusiasm, and sheer *joie de vivre* than I felt it deserved.

It was this quality, this abundance of gratitude over garden excess that made me truly understand the meaning of closed cycle. This garden with chickens was the first that had not been a burden for me. In the six or seven gardens before, there always had been vegetables out of control. Too many beans, zucchini big as baseball bats, chard choking out the weeds. Even though we harvested enough to last us through winter and beyond, I always went into each winter feeling I had abused this abundance somehow by failing to use everything. When the chickens began consuming the spoiled food with such gusto that it seemed, even to me, as if I had intended it for them all along, then I realized that gardens produce guilt. And chickens forgive it.

Why has no one explained this? This is the cycle: guilt and forgiveness, not food and fertilizer. I waited all that first summer and fall for my chickens to outgrow this zest and become jaded and ungrateful. But never. No chicken ever strolled with catlike reserve to see what I brought was worth its time. They always ran to me. Nothing was ever too ordinary for them.

Geoff Waite helped me carry out several buckets of garden guilt to them one evening. We stood watching their excited scrambling for a few minutes. "You know," Geoff said hesitantly. He was leaning over the fence, face furrowed as he struggled to phrase his thought. "You know," he repeated. I waited. "You know, Kant says, 'If you would look in the eye of stupidity, look into the eye of a chicken.'"

I looked into the eye of a chicken. The chicken looked back with interest.

THE FORESTER

CHAPTER FOUR

THE FORESTER

We used to know a couple in Asheville, North Carolina, who were living myths. The husband was a motorcycle repairman who learned his skills from *Zen and the Art of Motorcycle Maintenance*, or he kept the book so handy and visible I assumed I was supposed to think he was Zen trained. The wife was a weaver who produced art, not craft. She hung her tapestries in riotous display all over the house, each beautifully colored, but I never saw one without thinking of organs during surgery. Perhaps this was her intent, as they were organic gardeners, and organic carpenters, and organic vegetarians, with a perfectly mannered organic baby just learning to crawl. She knew healing through foot massage. He created their furniture. They had exquisite taste in music, cheese, and wine. They read books. They had no TV. They had a friend named Ed.

Ed, they said, had built a log cabin out of trees he cut and shaped himself and with metal he may have dug and forged himself. He set stones alone, drove nails with his fingertips, trapped raccoons with baling twine, they said. This all made me very nervous. Living myths have always made me nervous. So when the forester showed up at our Iowa farm that first summer and seemed to introduce himself as a living myth, he made me nervous.

Not so Mark. Mark idolized the forester, but then he had also loved the Asheville couple and kept writing them letters they never answered. He was upset—though I was pleased—to learn later via channels that the Asheville man had quit repairing zencycles and was now selling sunglasses from a Toyota. This is not to say I didn't appreciate all we learned from the forester. This is just to say he made me nervous.

The forester did not look like a myth. He was not seven feet tall or muscled enough to fell a tree with one swipe of an ax.

In fact, he was short, pot-bellied, with glasses, and had a beard so dense it was impossible to tell if his face was handsome or homely. He drove an ordinary two-door car, and his voice was thin.

He was cautious. He began by asking us broad questions to probe how we felt about the land, what we wanted to do with it. Mark said our goal was to use the land well, to produce income without abusing it.

"Do you want livestock?" the forester asked.

"Perhaps a few meat animals and a dairy cow," Mark said.

"Are you interested in wildlife habitat?"

"Definitely," Mark said.

The forester sorted this out silently, sizing us up. It was impossible to guess what he might be thinking behind that massive beard. Abruptly he suggested we go for a walk.

We had barely stepped out the kitchen door when he bent down and plucked a lawn weed, the ubiquitous one with oval leaves, parallel veins, and unmowable center stalk. "Plantain," he said. "In the spring the leaves are terrific in salads or cooked as greens." Mark's eyes opened wide. That a weed had a use was a new idea to him.

Just past the garden gate, the forester stopped again. "Taste this," he said, handing us a pale green clump of cloverlike leaves. "Suck on the leaves. Don't chew." It was sour, like sucking on a lemon, but sweet too, fresh-tasting. "This is wood sorrel," he said. "It has more vitamin C than most plants you can name, including the lemon it tastes like. It's terrific in salads and even better if you come across it on a hot day's hike. Some people call it hiker's tonic."

Mark bent over to gather a handful. "Don't use too much," the forester cautioned. "Too much over time can cause your bones to weaken. It interferes with calcium absorption." Mark drew back.

The forester continued in this manner, alert for plants. The grass in the fields was a mixture of timothy and brome. The weeds in front of the barn were spearmint, an excellent tea or flavoring for jellies and sauces. All mints, he said, from catnip to peppermint, had square stems. Did we know that thyme, sage, rosemary, and marjoram were mints? The low-growing garden weed, the intractable one with shiny striped flowers and geraniumlike leaves, that was cheese. Cheese leaves were good as a cooked green or a thickener for stews. The wheel-shaped fruits were good to nibble straight or add to salads. Cheeses were mallows.

"Like marshmallows?" Mark teased.

"The marsh mallow is an east coast plant that grows in salt marshes. Its roots were the original campfire marshmallow. Other important mallows are cotton, hollyhocks, and okra," the forester said.

Mark was so astonished to learn there was such a thing as an "original marsh mallow" he was silent. The fields about us were thick with Queen Anne's lace in bloom. "Have you ever seen a carrot in flower?" the forester asked. We hadn't. Queen Anne's lace was wild carrot, but like domestic carrot, it was a biennial. The root tasted best if harvested the first year, which meant to gather it you had to identify it by the leaves.

"So?" I said.

"So the leaves look so much like fool's parsley and poison hemlock that I would never try to harvest it. Too risky. Some people can tell the difference, but I can't. Caraway is another carrotlike plant that grows wild around here."

"Is real parsley a carrot?" I asked.

"I don't know," the forester said.

Another plant much in flower in our fields was a fuzzy, gray-green stalk with a yellow spike up the center. Common mullein—another biennial, another tea. A bush in a ravine that had flowered profusely in spring was elderberry; the berries were great if ripe and cooked properly and awful if unripe or uncooked. They were best in jams, muffins, or wine. Orange daylilies, blooming by a ditch, were edible, the forester said. The spring shoots could be used in salads or cooked like asparagus. The flowerbuds could be prepared like green beans. The flowers when fresh could be dipped in batter and fried like fritters; when withered or dried they could season stews. Young spring tubers could be added raw to salads; old tubers could be cooked like corn.

A nasty-looking thistle caught the forester's eye next. This was bull thistle—a great survival food next time we were lost in our yard. The roots of young plants, those without stems, could be eaten raw. The stems of older plants could be peeled and eaten raw.

"Not sure I want to do the peeling," I said.

"You really ought to chop those down," the forester said. "They're a noxious weed in the Iowa code because cattle won't eat them and they take over a pasture."

Nearby was burdock, which I'd always called cocklebur and the neighbors called sandbur. The leaves made a good cooked green in spring, the roots a vegetable, and the flower stalks a candy.

"Here's a mint," I said. "See the square stem?"

"Don't touch it." The forester yanked back my arm. "That's a stinging nettle. The hairs on the leaves will raise welts on your skin."

"Finally," Mark said, "a useless weed."

"Far from it," the forester said. "The top leaves are delicious steamed a few minutes or added to soups and stews. The stinging disappears when you cook them. They're rich in vitamins A and C, iron, and protein. Nutritionally, nettles are superior to most garden foods." The forester had been looking around as he spoke. "I don't see one here now, but if you do touch a nettle, there's a plant called the touch-me-not, or jewelweed, which will take the sting out."

"This is a plant I know," I said. "Milkweed."

"Don't destroy any milkweed. It's the only host of the monarch butterfly," the forester said.

"Does it have any food uses?" Mark asked.

"Cooked right, milkweed shoots can be asparagus. The flowers, fritters. The leaves, flowerbuds, and seedpods, vegetables. Make sure the sap is milky when you pick it or it's not milkweed."

"What do you mean 'cooked right'?" I asked.

"Change the water several times."

The vines on the paddock fence were wild grape, he told us. The fruit could be used any way domestic grapes were, and the unripe fruit was useful as pectin or thickener for jellies. The young leaves were good boiled as a green or used to wrap rice or meat for baking. "Don't confuse wild grape with moonseed; moonseed is poisonous. They're easy to tell apart though. Moonseed doesn't have any tendrils."

There were several mulberry trees by the paddock. "Are mulberries okay to eat?" I asked.

"The ripe ones are. Don't eat the unripe ones—they're hallucinogenic."

"So why aren't all the college kids trying to get high on mulberries?" Mark asked.

"Maybe they're not that hallucinogenic," the forester said with a wry tone that made me glance at him closely. As we approached the east pasture I raced ahead to find a spot I'd discovered a few days earlier. A nondescript spot in spring, it had suddenly exploded into color in summer. It contained occasional stands of purple aster surrounded by broad sweeps of a calf-high plant with whorled yellow flowers and lacy leaves. The color was butter-rich, reminiscent of a field of daffodils, but more intense, thicker. These plants rustled in the breeze like cellophane and grew untended, unplanted, and unseen, mostly because the spot was hidden from house or road. "What is this?" I asked.

"Partridge pea."

"What's it used for?"

"Nothing."

"Nothing?"

"Even goats won't eat it."

"A useless plant?"

"Well, it's a legume. It's a good soil builder."

"He's saying there's no such thing as a useless plant, Pat," Mark said.

"Poison ivy is pretty useless," the forester corrected. His thin voice took on that wry edge again, which I found very charming.

His tone was so disarming, I immediately suspected he never ate wild vegetables himself. I became convinced of it. This was a man who liked his beans domesticated. Here he'd made Mark so excited by wild edibles I was sure I'd be peeling thistles and boiling roots through dozens of water changes all the next day. The forester was just setting us up, I thought.

"Do you like New Zealand spinach?" I asked him. This was a test question I'd invented — for measuring living myths. New Zealand spinach was a heat-resistant vegetable I grew occasionally. Most spinach "bolts" or goes to seed when the weather turns hot, but this plant keeps producing. Few people then had heard of it. The forester hadn't either. That's why I created the question — to see how people reacted to new information. Living myths are never curious about what other people know. They need to overwhelm the rest of us, to know more than we do, and one way they make sure we have nothing to teach them is not to listen to us. To my surprise, though, the forester was curious; he wanted to know about the spinach. A point in his favor. That wry tone, a healthy curiosity — maybe there was more to this myth than usual.

The walk that day forever changed the way I look at fields. They no longer seemed monochromatic with grass. I saw the pasture become and stay overwhelmingly diverse, even after several years of toting field guides. Rare was the walk when someone didn't find a plant new to me and smash my expert pose with an earnest "What's this?" The forester rarely had to say "I don't know," of course.

The forester lived in the woods, of course.

"Of course. Of course, a forester would live in the woods," was Mark's comment.

"Hell," said the forester in that wry tone I liked. "We've only lived in the woods since April." Before then he and his family lived in an apartment overlooking the Mississippi River, right on a bend. For years he'd endured barge traffic in his bedroom. "Half a dozen times a night, those damn foghorns blare and those damn klieg lights swing back and forth, lighting up the walls over the bed while those boats negotiate that damn turn. Great for birth control," he said.

Among stories like this he also cautiously told us he and his wife were building their forest home themselves out of materials they'd salvaged themselves with tools, some of which they'd built themselves. They'd been working on it, one nail at a time, for two years. It was a long way from finished, but at least this spring they could move in. There were no klieg lights in the woods, he said.

Most of the materials for the house came from buildings they tore down. The oak flooring had come from a carriage house, the bathtub from a farmhouse, the windows from a school, studs from a firehouse, joists from a barn, tin roof from another barn, the wood furnace from our house.

"Our house?" said Mark.

"Yep. The widow wanted to install an oil furnace. . . . "

"The year oil prices went up, I bet," said Mark.

"And she said if I got it out of there I could have it. I jumped at the chance. The furnace had me worried that I might actually have to buy something." Only the house trusses were new, he said. He would drive around looking for abandoned buildings and offer to tear them down in exchange for salvage. Right now he was looking for a barn with a stone foundation. He wanted the stone for a hearth and solar storage mass.

What he didn't salvage he swapped for. He had made his insulation by shredding and chemically treating old newspapers. He'd swapped firewood to get the chemicals.

What he didn't salvage or swap for, he invented. He was particularly proud of one tool he'd designed, a board tightener he'd used to lay flooring. The house design was his own invention, too. He described it as a giant, semisolar chicken coop. The north wall had a row of screening running at foot level, and the south wall had a similar row at ceiling level to create cooling air currents in summer. The awnings for the south windows were pulled up in winter to let more light in the windows and cover the screening.

Indoor shutters closed the windows on winter nights. The water system was energy-intensive too. All waste water was recycled into the deep bed garden. Most household water was collected from the roof and stored in a cistern. Drinking water came from a well he'd drilled himself.

There seemed to be no limit to the man's ingenuity. Even the land was acquired in an innovative way. He'd learned that before the turn of the century it had been either custom or law that every farm was entitled to a woodlot. Since the best wood grew near rivers, most farm woodlots were several miles from their farms. When wood was no longer used for fuel, many families forgot they owned an acre or two on a stream somewhere. The forester spent several years tracking down heirs of these forgotten parcels. Most didn't know about the land and didn't mind letting it go cheaply. He'd put together forty acres this way.

Mark thought the forester was the most interesting person he'd ever met. It wasn't just that he was clever. Mark admired his values too. The forester had two sons, identical twins, and one problem with twins is remembering they're individuals. So he was helping each boy build a tree house in the woods. "It will be his. He can go there and be alone if he wants, and he'll learn skills by working on it." Mark liked that. The forester's values put him slightly at odds with local ideas in some ways too. Mark liked that also. Once the forester had gone door to door asking the farmers in the county not to be so neat in their mowing, but to leave weeds growing here and there for wildlife habitat.

"And?" said Mark.

"And they about laughed me into the ground," the forester said.

No wonder the man was so cautious. And no wonder he liked us. Our fields and ditches were a mess. Mark didn't mention that this was because we were so inept with machines we couldn't keep a mower running. So I mentioned it. "Don't think we're wildlife nuts," I said. "We're messy because we're incompetent."

The forester said he could tell that.

Yes, I guess I liked him, even if he was a myth. He had a sense of humor, a quality I'd never before encountered in a living myth.

Like Mark, the forester had grown up in a city, a tough part of East St. Louis, he told us over dinner at his house a few days after that walk. He had impulsively invited us over and showed us his woods, including eighty-three white oak trees carefully numbered with red paint, which when harvested would probably pay off the mortgage on the land. He also showed us his Willoughby tractor. Willoughby was the pig, full name Willoughby Porkchop, or as one of the twins patiently explained to us, "You know, Willoughby, Will-o-Be, Will be Porkchop." They fed the pig corn chips donated by a sister-in-law who worked for a Frito-Lay plant. Willoughby's job was to root up his pen vigorously. Every few weeks, the family would move the pen, leaving behind a perfectly tilled and fertilized garden bed.

The house was everything we had imagined. The forester showed us the automatic-sealing doors, which shut tight with the help of old window weights. He showed us the pipes that led bathwater (but not dishwater) straight to the garden. He showed us the composting toilet. Upstairs was a normal commode minus a flush tank. To flush, one simply dumped a handful of sawdust down the hole. Below was a special bin complete with turncrank and viewglass, where we stood for a few minutes solemnly admiring the family turds.

Yes, the house was a marvel. The family, however, was not what I expected. The wife at first seemed as living a myth as any. That is, she did not care to learn from us neophytes. I remember trying to say something about canning; I'd been canning for six years by then and felt I was an associate myth at least. But she bluntly let me know I could tell her nothing new. So I switched roles; I became the seeker. Myths love describing their discoveries and lore; most are delighted if you want your head filled with naturalness and self-sufficiency. But, no, she didn't care to share the family canning secrets. She left me at a loss for conversation. In fact, she avoided conversation entirely.

That's not to say she was quiet. Far from it. She began before we were even in the house to berate its looks. The kitchen cabinets were not just so; this especially bothered her. I had to agree—the cabinets were not K-Mart perfect. They were rugged, raw, and, I thought, charming for it. Besides, purchased cabinets would look silly in the woods. Why was she apologizing? Her fussing—first about the cabinets, then about her furniture and dishes—puzzled me. It was not the fussing itself; this I saw as the traditional hostess pose, the "forgive this humble home" routine women have inflicted on guests for centuries.

It was the terms of her embarrassment that puzzled me. The ideal against which she criticized her forest home seemed to be suburban prefab. Then just as I'd decided she was out of place in a handmade home, she would begin talking about her crafts, sounding more back-to-the-country fanatic than the Asheville couple, or the forester.

I couldn't make sense of this at all. I remember sitting outside, very late, swapping stories, good stories, while the twins were in bed, when I became sharply aware of the shape of the house. It loomed a trapezoid blackness against the moonlit sky. On the table a candle flickered. I noticed the table had been hand-built from scraps of wood, and autumn leaves had been layered into the varnish. It seemed very beautiful and I said so. "It's nothing, a scrap. It's not a real picnic table," the wife said. What did she consider real? I wondered. A kit from Sears? Suddenly I felt very alert, as if I had heard a whippoorwill. There was something about her apologies that seemed very important, a clue to something I needed to know. But the perception slipped away. It would be several years before I'd think again of her need for real picnic tables. But the next time I would understand it.

BISCUIT

CHAPTER FIVE

BISCUIT

Mark became infatuated with the forester. Before the forester, Mark's vision of the farm was lyrical, yes, but focused, no. The truth was, we had no idea how to change our vague aesthetic into a real farm. But after the forester, Mark could see. He had details, goals.

He woke up talking about the forester's rainwater-collection system the morning after dinner at his house. It was an exhilarating new idea for Mark, although the forester had told us it was an approach thousands of years old and still used by most of the world. While I was making coffee, Mark went outside to study our roof and returned minutes later, excited to have discovered that the roof once collected water. All the gutters focused toward a single collection point ending right above the cistern. It must have been disconnected when the windmill was set up. Mark wanted to hook the gutters to the cistern right away.

I hesitated. "Wait until the well fails," I said. Mark didn't seem to hear me. He simply asked again later would I try to find a welder who could connect the gutter to the cistern.

I said we didn't need it. We had pure cold well water, so soft we were the only country family I knew without a softener. As long as our water was so good, why mix it with dirty rainwater full of insects and bird droppings from the roof?

Patiently he explained we would let the roof wash a few minutes before shunting the flow into the cistern; that's why the gutter terminal had a **Y** joint.

"But we work," I said. "What if we're not home and it rains and the cistern overflows?"

"So we keep it shunted outside when we're gone, just like we keep the windmill off now."

"But what if we miss a rainstorm and it doesn't rain again for six weeks?"

"We'll keep the windmill hooked up for emergencies."

"But since we have the windmill, why bother?"

"Because it's a beautiful idea."

It was always gentle, this debate, but neither of us seemed inclined to yield. Fortunately, another beautiful idea intervened. The forester had told us we should get some geese since we kept chickens. Chickens were so stupid they would sit quietly and let a fox or coyote kill them one by one. Geese would raise a racket to wake you to come to the rescue, although if the intruder was anything smaller than a mountain lion, the geese would probably chase the varmint off before you could find your shoes or shotgun. Besides, the forester told us, geese made terrific watchdogs. He knew of a factory in town that had kept Dobermans as sentries but was still robbed repeatedly. When the owners acquired a flock of geese, the robberies stopped. Geese were like dogs, he said — they knew who their owners were. But unlike dogs, who often licked the hands of visiting thieves, geese chased strangers and packed a mean bite. We both began to like this picture of a watch goose honking beneath the window.

A neighbor had a friend who had a neighbor who had a son who had a pair of geese he was willing to sell. After the appropriate grapevine linkages, our neighbor brought us two pure white and unbelievably enormous birds in a cage. "This is a fifty-year commitment," the neighbor said. "Geese can live that long. They mate for life. I can't tell them apart, but the male will be the one who gets on top." By now, all the neighbors assumed we had to be told things like this. We'd already read a number of articles about the affectionate fidelity of geese; it was a rare goose that would remate if it lost its first mate. People were also fond of geese because they were grass eaters and so could help weed a garden. "Shut them up for a few days until they get used to this place as home. Then you can let them out," the neighbor advised.

The birds were quiet as we carried them to the corncrib. I was most surprised by the color of their eyes, an intense blue; the one I carried kept twisting its head to examine me, first with one lovely eye, then the other. "I think I can tell them apart," I told Mark. "I think the one you're carrying is the male. He has a big bump on his nose." We stuck them in the crib, gave them food and water, and talked to them for a while. They looked us over closely, studying everything about us. We named the male Bruce and the female Biscuit.

At dinner time we heard an incredible uproar from the corncrib and ran out to see what raccoon, coyote, or burglar the geese had surprised. The uproar was Biscuit screaming for her life because Bruce was beating her. He was holding her neck in his beak and whapping her with his wings. At dusk, the uproar resumed: Bruce beating Biscuit again. At dawn he beat her again. At midmorning. At noon. Any time she approached the food or water he attacked her. I tried putting the buckets of food and water at opposite ends of the crib so he could guard only one at a time. His solution was to corner Biscuit and beat her if she moved at all.

"Do you suppose they're unhappily married?" I asked Mark.

"I think they're just upset at being locked up," he said.

We let them out and they went directly to the pond. Perhaps they smelled it. Surely they couldn't see it, for the grass was over their heads. They began running when they saw the water, plunged in, splashing ecstatically, and became exquisitely graceful. I'd never seen a goose before; I've yet to see a swan. But watching them stretch their wings and arch their necks, I couldn't imagine how a swan could be more lovely than these two ordinary geese. The pair floated, preened, and grazed contentedly from then on, except when Bruce beat Biscuit, which was as often as he could catch her.

When they weren't fighting, they made a grand sight, and I enjoyed coming upon the pond and seeing them there. Sometimes I could see the duo from my study window too. But a pond pastoral was not what Mark had in mind. His vision was of a goose honking beneath the window. He wanted the birds up here at the house, not down there. After some days of deliberating what to do, he invented a goose rouster. This device consisted of a hundred feet or so of rope, with milk jugs placed so they would rattle against each other. His plan was to stretch the rope across the pond and together we would walk around the pond toward each other, pulling it tighter and tighter, rattling it, until the geese would be forced on land where we could catch them.

We had lots of milk jugs because we saved them for gardening. I wished we'd had fewer because Mark insisted on perfection, which meant using all the jugs and tying them at precise intervals. When this tedious work was done, we walked over to the pond, but the goose rouster rattled so loudly the geese looked at each other and smoothly stole from the water while we were yards away. Mark ran and managed to catch Biscuit, but Bruce headed over the back of the dam into a ravine and from there into a neighboring pond that was not a pond but a swamp. A dark swamp. A swamp surrounded on all sides by steep, unclimbable banks covered with briars and thorn bushes and spiders and poison roaches and vicious snakes. Maybe even ghosts. A mean pond. And our goose was in it.

We put Biscuit in the corncrib and went back to study the darkness. "Maybe if we walk over that cornfield to the east we could get down that right bank," Mark ventured. On an aerial map our land seemed to be at the center of an inexplicable occurrence of badlands streaked by ravines but surrounded by flat fields. It was impossible to cross from one end of our land to the other without resorting to road or cornfields. In other words, it was a long walk to that right bank. By the time we got there, Bruce had decided he was a free goose and was sitting on the shore.

"You keep him in sight. Tell me if he moves," Mark said, and began creeping down the ravine, freezing into place whenever he stepped on a twig. Bruce would lift his head when he heard the crackling in the bushes, but he did not leave the shore. After a time, I could see Mark. He was close, yet Bruce still had not seen him. Mark waited, choosing his moment. The moment came. He surged from the brush, arms over his head, and dove. Bruce, bawling at top voice, flailing his wings, ran out on the surface of the water—truly, *running* on the water's surface; I watched in disbelief—and reached the other side, leaving Mark splayed in the mud and cursing, cursing so angrily I was frightened for him. Abruptly the cursing stopped. His silence was chilling. "Pat?" Mark said. His tone was anguished. "What do you see on that bank over there?"

I saw two white geese.

I felt we'd left reality and entered a dream. I was still recovering from having seen a goose walk on water, and now I was being asked to believe I saw two geese where there should have been one. The image stayed solid. There were two geese on that bank. They looked at us with the confident air that comes to people or geese who know they are in control of the situation. "Maybe one of the neighbors has lost a goose in this swamp, too," I said.

"I don't think so," said Mark.

Biscuit was gone from the corncrib, of course. Mark's first reaction was to blame me, but then he remembered that he'd latched the door, and we both were sure it had been secure. She had accomplished the goose equivalent of bending the bars and knotting the sheets. We stood in glum silence. "Any ideas?" Mark said finally.

"Let's go back to the house and untie milk jugs," I said.

So the geese stayed in the swamp, even further from honking beneath the window than before. We'd hear them from time to time and assume Bruce was beating Biscuit again.

Then one afternoon we got a frantic phone call from our next-door neighbor. We hardly knew her. The country is odd that way. We knew almost all our neighbors except the ones closest to us. She was mildly hysterical. There was a goose loose on the road. Was it ours? We drove over right away. I was shocked to see her standing on her porch literally guarding her two children. She stood holding her toddlers behind her with one hand, the other hand in front of her, ready to ward off the goose beyond. It was Biscuit, who to me looked tired and dirty, not dangerous.

When Biscuit saw us, she halfheartedly jumped in the drainage ditch. Mark jumped in after her and caught her easily. By now he was tired of doing all the goose jumping, and he muttered to me, "Where the hell were you?" Then he handed me the goose. Her neck had several raw spots where Bruce had bitten the feathers off. "It wasn't the swamp she left," I said. "She left *him*."

By now most of our friends were aware of Bruce and Biscuit's difficulties and had much to say about this new development. "She left him, good for her"; "If Biscuit needs it, I can refer her to a battered wives' shelter"; "Why don't you get them a marriage counselor?" And so on. A sociologist friend of ours told us that wife beating is a major problem in rural areas. Farmers feel they have no control over the weather or prices so they take it out on their wives; they feel helpless and try to get control by hurting someone else.

We put Biscuit in the corncrib again, figuring the best way to tame her was with food. She would not eat, we decided, unless she took it from our hands. The first day we held out alfalfa and clover to her. She looked at it, looked at us, looked at it, looked at us. We talked to her, cooing actually. "You're so hungry and this looks so good, c'mon, you want it, yes, you do, come here and get it, that's all you have to do." Finally she ran over and snatched some. On the third day, instead of snatching and running, she snuggled down between us and took turns taking food from each of us.

"I think this goose is tame," Mark said. Thereafter she would always come over to us when she saw us and beg for a handout. All we might do was pluck a strand of grass from beside her, yet she'd treat this as if it were some grand delicacy. She followed us about like a puppy, curious about everything we did. Whenever I'd weed the garden, she'd be right there beside me, plucking out the grass while I got the other weeds. I discovered she didn't eat only grass. I was forced to cover the cabbages with chicken wire to protect them from her.

Mark became deeply attached to her and discovered he could

make her talk to him. She had a repertoire of thirty or forty sounds. Her side of the conversation was always loud, animated, convincing, and funny—Biscuit clearly liked people. At a lawn picnic once, she approached one of our guests, who was sitting on the grass, and began an animated conversation. "What does she want?" the friend asked, laughing.

"Your coleslaw," I said.

He held out a forkful of coleslaw to her, and she accepted gracefully. He fed her all he had, exclaiming with each forkful, "I don't believe this."

Because we had closed the garden gate to keep her from getting to the pond, Mark put a tub by the cistern under the controversial gutter terminal to catch rainwater for her. "Ssh, come here," he said to me one morning in the kitchen. She had climbed in the tub. She sat there, filling it completely and trying to look dignified, even though she knew she was absurd. Biscuit made us laugh a lot, and we may have wounded her pride with our laughter. The expression "silly goose" must have begun with one like her.

One morning I looked out my study window and saw a goose on our pond. "Bruce is back," I called to Mark. He came to the window. "Couldn't stay away from her, eh?" he said. This time we designed a quieter goose rouster and succeeded in driving him to land on our side of the dam. But he could run a lot faster than Biscuit. Even in high grass he was outrunning both of us, darting and zigzagging and evading us until finally he began to tire and Mark saw his chance. He dove. It was a stupendous dive, like O. J. Simpson stretching for an extra half yard. The two wrestled arm to wing, until Mark pinned Bruce. Then he rose slowly from the ground, holding the bird. "Where the hell were you?" he asked once again.

We tried the food-taming routine with Bruce, but at the end of a week of talking and cooing, Bruce was still snatching and running. To save time, Mark and I took turns feeding him, me in the morning, Mark in the afternoon. At the end of two weeks, no change. At the end of four weeks we gave up. But then we had to decide whether to put Bruce with Biscuit. During the four weeks since his return, Biscuit had come daily to the fence and called to Bruce. The two would talk back and forth a while, working it out, it seemed to me. She appeared truly to miss him.

"Are you sure you want him back?" I asked her. She was sure. So we let him in the yard. He seemed content most of the time, but he never took handouts or talked to us. He splashed in the tub and would follow us at a distance, although I think he was following Biscuit rather than us. Most of the time he was calm. But every once in a while something would snap in him; he'd lose control and take a bite out of Biscuit. She seemed resigned to it.

So were we, and as far as our own differences were concerned, as long as the geese were alive to play in the tub, Mark never again mentioned hooking up the gutter to the cistern. This meant I did not have to think about it. I'd realized, if not acknowledged, that more than water was at issue. There was a fundamental difference in the way we each saw the place. The cistern/gutter controversy was only the first of many similar disagreements—Mark would be eager for some idea, and I'd be reserved. On this front, however, there was peace, if geese honking beneath a window can be called peace.

TREE FARM

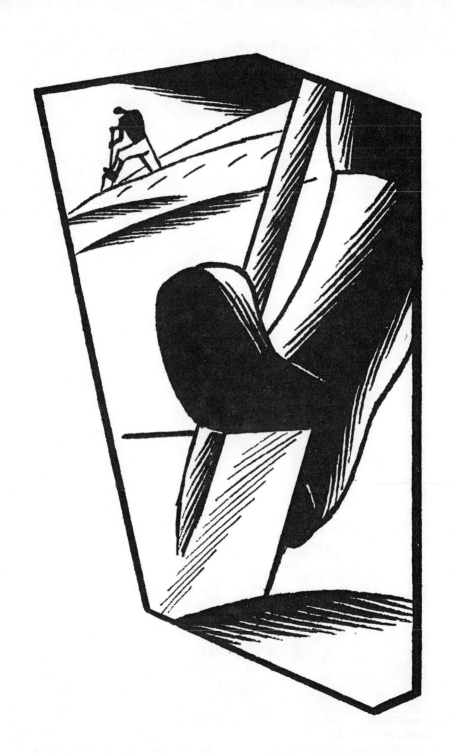

CHAPTER SIX

TREE FARM

The idea that we become tree farmers was the forester's, of course. True to pattern, Mark was immediately enthusiastic, while I had reservations. We'd asked the forester where we could get wood for the stove we were installing. What was wrong with our woods? he asked. I told him I didn't want to cut it down and spoil the view. He said we had enough land to grow lumber and ten times the land we needed for firewood; if we harvested right, we could heat our home with wood forever.

I have trouble believing words like "forever"; Mark chided me sharply for saying so. He too was noticing our pattern. My endless skepticism troubled him. The forester, on the other hand, seemed to enjoy having to sell me on each new idea. Quick converts like Mark were no challenge. He took us to a hill in the woods, searched for a minute or two, and found a stand of small oaks. "How old do you think those trees are?" he asked.

"Ten years, maybe fifteen," I said. The largest of the clump was about eighteen feet high and as thick as my arm.

"They're five years old. I recorded when they sprouted," he said.

I didn't believe him. "My mother has a nineteen-year-old tree on the lawn that's no bigger than that," I said. Mark noted my rudeness with an upraised eyebrow, but said nothing.

"Your parents planted a seedling. This is a sprout." The forester pawed in the leaves at the base of the clump and exposed an almost rotted stump. Most hardwoods had the ability to resprout after the crown was cut, he said. Dormant buds between the rings in the trunk sprouted after the tree was cut. Because they drew on the mature tree's root system, they grew very quickly, maybe three, four, five times faster than a seedling. "Look behind you," he said.

Behind us was a hillside of young black-locust trees.

"Oaks, maples, poplars, ash, hickories, fruit trees, all sprout from stumps. But locust trees can sprout from roots. Somewhere at the center of that grove is an old locust stump."

"Are the young trees feeding on the old tree's roots?" I asked.

"And putting out new ones," the forester said.

"So the tree doesn't die when it's cut."

The forester laughed. "We applied scientists usually don't think of trees in terms of individual lives and deaths."

"She does," Mark said. "She doesn't go so far as to name them. . ."

"He's saying I've been known to talk to them," I said.

"You should, you should," the forester said.

"But my point—if a tree is never cut, it has a life cycle, right? Seedling, youth, maturity, old age, death?"

"Right."

"If it's cut, though, it regenerates."

"It can."

"Which means if we cut down a tree we've given it immortal life."

"Whew," the forester said. Mark laughed.

My mind began to run away with the idea. I liked the idea of being a tree's savior, bringing it life everlasting through death, being an oak's archangel Gabriel: "Hail sapling, full of grace," and getting a winter's yield for my servitude. If trees, not man, were the species destined for immortality, then our technological destiny was not the computer but the chain saw.

If that were the divine plan, it had gone awry, the forester said. A key ecological crisis in most of the Third World was deforestation. The loss of trees was changing the climate, decreasing world rainfall, creating deserts, and undermining subsistence economies. The problem was not too many people for too little wood. The bigger problem was that most world cultures had forgotten about sprouting. The technique for managing tree growth through sprout regeneration was called sustained yield, or short rotation, or coppicing, the forester said. Using coppice with poplars could produce 103 tons of firewood per acre over ten years. Conventional management might produce only 12 tons an acre in a decade.

Now it was Mark's turn not to believe. "Is that true?" he said.

"Indeed yes. Because we have a climate suitable for hardwoods in this country, we have the potential to be the Saudi Arabia of wood."

"Neither of you are answering my question," I said. "Do trees have souls?"

"Coppicing is an old, old technique," the forester said. I thought he hadn't heard me. "The earliest written reference to it I know of is in some thirteenth-century British manuscripts, but it was ancient in Britain even then."

"Britain. Druids. Tree worshippers," Mark said.

"Right. And Britain's Forest of Dean is still producing firewood while the Cedars of Lebanon are long gone. The ancient Britons had an intuitive understanding of coppicing, and obviously the Druids thought trees had souls."

I giggled, imagining what the neighbors would think if I told them I was a Druid.

"Tell them you're a coppicer," the forester said. "Same thing."

"A tree cop," said Mark.

The forester smiled. "That might not be a bad idea. A crime problem down in this part of the state is tree rustling."

"What?" I said.

"How could anyone rustle a tree?" Mark said.

"If you ever see a chain saw with a muffler on it bigger than the saw, you're seeing a rustler's saw."

"But why would anyone steal a tree?"

"Lumber. A mature black walnut tree, especially from around here, can be worth one or two thousand dollars for furniture. We get inquiries from furniture makers all over the world who want Iowa black walnut."

"I thought this was a corn state," I said.

"Not around the rivers," the forester said.

"How old is mature?" Mark asked.

"Thirty years."

"Oh, is that all."

I was thinking about a thousand dollars a tree. "I want to raise black walnuts," I said.

"I want to rustle them," Mark said.

So we became tree farmers. Under the forester's direction we ordered two thousand tree seedlings—black walnut, green ash, and autumn olive. The green ash was to serve as a trap tree; insects and deer would prefer to nibble ash over walnut, in theory, and so leave the walnuts alone. The autumn olive was to feed the walnuts, since it was a nitrogen fixer.

To coppice, we would cut trees in winter as close to the ground as possible to maximize sprouting. Then we were to thin the sprouts every three years to assure that some reached firewood size rather than remaining thin and brushy. And we needed to plan a twenty-year rotation system so that each site would be cut only once in twenty years. Mark and I both had trouble taking the proper stance toward that twenty-year plan. We were poring over graph paper one night trying to draw and date twenty sites. Mark stopped at about 1992. "This is absurd?" It was a question, not a statement.

"I wonder why they call it short rotation?" I said.

"Maybe twenty years is shorter than one hundred," Mark said.

"You do learn to think differently about time when you raise trees, don't you?" I said.

Time was not our only philosophical hurdle. I spent most of the winter before the seedlings arrived fretting. No other task we'd set for ourselves seemed as formidable as this one. Garden beds, wood stoves, solar greenhouse, goats—nothing seemed to compare to the enormity of planting two thousand trees by hand. Our land was too rugged to consider tree-planting equipment. I calculated if we worked ten-hour days, each of us could plant fifty trees a day. Thus, the two of us could complete the task in twenty days. Mark and I both were teaching then. Teachers do not take vacations in April. I lost sleep over this and wanted to cancel the order.

"We'll get help," Mark said.

I reminded him of my brother, who had sharply changed the

subject when we mentioned we needed help moving the freezer in the basement; of the friend who had agreed to help us repair our chimney, then developed an acute fear of heights once he got up there and had to be coaxed down; of the five friends who had volunteered to help us move when we bought this farm, two of whom actually showed up, one of whom arrived announcing a sudden bad back; of the friend who offered to help us dig garden beds but who arrived with a new Chinese kite, so we flew the kite—and enjoyed ourselves. No regrets there. But the pattern had made me fearful of projects that needed friends. The thought that we needed about ten willing friends for this one did nothing to improve my sleep.

Then a friend told us how she'd enjoyed her Girl Scout troop's project each summer of replanting burned forests. She was eager to help. Another said he'd never planted trees before but it "sounded fun." And my mother shocked me by begging to come from Chicago to help. I did not ask her. I don't think I even hinted we needed help. During one of our what's-new phone calls I merely mentioned we'd ordered trees, and she began bubbling with interest: "Wonderful fun. When? Promise me you'll tell me so I can be there."

"Don't worry," I said, suddenly unsure if this was *my* mother I was talking to; had I dialed the wrong number? For reasons I didn't understand I was finding tree planters easier to engage than freezer toters. Even so, the April tree-arrival date approached and I still felt short of help. The forester told us to call Steve Atherton, the county conservationist; county conservationists, among many things, planted trees for a living.

I was reluctant to call a stranger, especially to ask him to volunteer for a busman's holiday. So I didn't telephone him until Mark and I ran out of acquaintances to ask. Steve cut me off in the middle of my "help us" spiel by first, agreeing to come; second, offering to bring two other men to help; and third, asking us if we needed shovels. Only then did he ask how many trees we had.

"Two thousand."

"Um, that's a lot," he said. I thought I heard backpedaling coming. "Now I've already promised someone else to help Saturday morning."

Yep, scratch one volunteer, I thought.

"So I won't get there until ten or so. That all right?"

I was relieved he was coming at all.

"Let's see," he went on, more thinking aloud than talking to me, "with your friends helping and the three of us—this will be a long session won't it?—we won't get done until after lunch, so I'll bring some sandwiches and. . ."

"After lunch?" I said.

"Yeah, with two thousand it's going to take a couple hours, even with six or seven people working. Maybe three hours."

"Three *hours?*"

"Well, you've never planted. I figure you can't do more than four hundred an hour, and me and the others we can do about seven hundred an hour but since some of this is in woods that'll slow us down hunting for sites, but I'd say. . ."

"Four *hundred* an hour?" I said.

"Well, maybe you can do more. I didn't mean to say you couldn't," Steve apologized.

I was so surprised I had stood up from my chair. Seldom have I experienced such a complete switch in perspective. I was looking at a commitment of hours, not days, if his numbers were right, and I was so afraid I'd heard wrong I had to ask Steve a couple of times if he was sure, really sure, trees could be planted so quickly by hand. He was sure. He planted trees for a living, he quietly reminded me. "Steve," I said. "Don't bring sandwiches. I'll *feed* you lunch."

Steve showed up as promised with two helpers—Gary and Greek—the shovels, his possibly part-Labrador dog Sam, and a stack of sandwiches. Prudence or distrust, I wondered of the sandwiches. They were anxious to get started. Gary took a bag of seedlings and poured a little water in it. The rest of us did the same. "Not so much," Steve said to Mark. "Don't drown them. Just keep them moist."

They started to disperse toward the woods. "Wait," I said to Steve. "How do you plant?"

He'd forgotten I was a beginner. "You make a slit like this," he said, plunging his shovel straight into the ground.

"So you're making a slit, not a hole?" I said.

"Right. Only you want it wider at the bottom than at the top, so rock your shovel back and forth a little, but not too much or it'll be hard to close. And make it deep enough. Slip a seedling in, but don't bend the roots up. If they bend, pull out and make your slit bigger. Roots must point down. If your slit is wide and deep enough they'll go right in. Then you whomp the slit closed with your heel."

He'd done it faster than he'd described it. I tried it. "No, *whomp*. Really bang the ground with your heel," he said. "You want to dent the turf. You're trying to close that slit at the bottom, all the way down."

I whomped. No dent.

"Well, here's a trick that doesn't take so much strength. You make another slit here parallel to the first one, rock your shovel so it presses the first slit closed." This was easier for me.

"Tramp it down a little anyway," Steve advised.

"Tramp, not whomp?" I said.

"Yeah. Just a little insurance to be sure you got the air pockets out."

"That's it?" I said. It was much easier than setting out garden plants.

"Be sure you put the seedling in to the same level it was before. See this change in color on the stem? That's the soil line. That's the level you want. Don't slip it in any deeper than that."

I tried it again. "Sink your shovel in straight. You don't want to plant at an angle." I reached to pull out the seedling. "No, that's okay. It'll straighten out. Just try to get most of them in straight, but—to tell the truth—I don't replant any unless the roots are bent. Maybe I should, you know?"

"Why bother getting them in straight?" I asked.

"Aesthetics. And straight trees make better lumber."

Mark headed off to work by himself on one hillside. Greek disappeared toward another. Both worked silently—I don't think I heard Greek say a word all day. Gary and Steve worked together, pausing in mid-sentences for the whomping effort but otherwise chatting all the time. Every ten minutes or so Steve would call his dog to keep it from wandering too far. His yell had an edge of resignation and hilarity, as if he were beginning to feel that forty million bellows to a dog were ten million too many. For all of five minutes I worked beside Gary and Steve, but they quickly outpaced me. The sounds of the chatter, the intermittent thuds of their heeling-in, the hoarse bellows for Sam receded by the minute.

Soon I was quite alone as I slit, rocked the shovel, slipped in seedlings, closed slits, and emptied my mind of everything but April. It seemed essential somehow that tree planting be done alone. In the end I never came close to Steve's four-hundred-an-hour estimate; two hundred an hour was more like it, but that was still far better than my fifty-a-day idea. We finished by midafternoon. Steve ate the lunch I prepared, and then having finished with mine, he ate the lunch he had brought. So it *was* prudence, I thought.

POISON

CHAPTER SEVEN

POISON

Our next philosophical crisis was more subtle and less easily resolved. It began the winter day we sat with the forester working on our tree plan. He had helped us choose tree species, worked out site and spacing options with us, and begun discussing preparing the ground. It took Mark and me a few minutes to realize that what he meant by "prepare the ground" was "use herbicides."

I was surprised; I didn't expect such a suggestion. Mark was horrified and interrupted, pushing away from the table as he spoke. "Never. I won't use poisons." The forester hardly paused; he didn't see the look in Mark's eye. He began to reason with Mark, totally unaware that the issue on the table suddenly was not herbicides, but trust.

"It's a trade-off with herbicides. Not using them encourages soil erosion. Use them and you handle chemicals. Which is the greater problem for you?" The forester had asked a reasonable question.

Mark said, "A neighbor told us that 2,4, something, T is Agent Orange."

"2,4,5-T?"

"Yeah. Is that true? Is it really Agent Orange?"

"Oh my," the forester said. He was suddenly choosing his words carefully. He was used to Mark trusting his advice. "It's a cousin to Agent Orange. The agent used in Vietnam was impure; 2,4,5-T is more refined. But I'm not telling you to use that. It's been banned by the EPA for one thing, and even if it hadn't, I still wouldn't recommend it. There are many herbicides, and these I'm telling you about are not so noxious."

"But they're still poisons. Isn't there another way?" Mark asked.

"Yes, mechanical control—mowing, cultivation. Whenever possible I recommend mowing for weed control in tree plantings. But here are the issues. The first year after transplanting, tree seedlings are very weak. They cannot compete with weeds for sunlight. If sunlight were the only problem, mowing might be enough. But root competition is a factor too. By the time weeds or grass have grown enough to be mowed, their roots may have damaged the seedlings. You can't cultivate near trees because their roots are too shallow. So what can you do? On flat ground I usually recommend for the first two or three years you treat a narrow band eighteen inches wide with herbicides. This is where you put your trees. Then you mow between the rows. This minimizes herbicide use and still gives the trees a chance. After three years you can stop the herbicide and just mow. After five years you can stop the mowing — the trees can take it from there.

"But in your case you've got steeply sloping land that has a serious erosion problem thanks to years of hogs rooting up the ground cover. Because it's so badly eroded now you couldn't get a riding mower or a tractor down in there. Some spots you couldn't even get a push mower in. So I'm suggesting you treat each tree site with herbicide for five years, three at least, and take your chances between the trees. If you don't treat, you might as well not plant, because weeds will kill your trees."

We were silenced by this.

"There's another issue in your case. Ignore the erosion problem. Let's talk reality. You both work. Could you mow your acreage twice weekly for the twelve weeks of summer? Would you, even if you could?"

He was right. We had neither time nor desire to be fanatically devoted to our trees. Here we sat, white-collar folk, clinging to both a horror of chemicals and a disapproval of poor soil management. It was easy to be righteous about farming when you don't farm. By choosing to plant, though, we became real farmers, tree farmers. This meant things were about to look a lot different to us. I also thought as he spoke how little I knew about herbicides. All my attitudes were based on scare articles in homesteading magazines, on the one hand, and those warm family-scene TV commercials for chemicals, on the other. Neither source was at all objective.

"It will be a tough decision for us," I said. "It hits right at fundamental values." I asked him for some things to read and promised we would read up on the subject before deciding. Mark nodded. At least this postponed a decision.

The first hurdle for me as I set about trying to sort out this issue was vocabulary. I had thought the word "pesticide" referred to insect pests. But I learned it is the general word to describe any agricultural chemical control agent from "plant regulator" to "plant killer." There were seventeen types listed by the EPA. "Insecticides" were for killing insects, though all copy called it "controlling." Miticides, acaricides, nematicides, fungicides, bacteriacides, rodenticides, avicides, piscicides, molluscicides, and predacides were for controlling mites, spiders, nematodes, fungi, bacteria, rodents, birds, fish, snails, and larger vertebrates—in that order.

"Repellents" were pesticides that did not kill but drove pests away; "attractants" were the opposite. "Plant growth regulators" changed plant growth, speeding it up or slowing it down instead of killing the plant outright. "Defoliants" removed leaves without killing immediately; "dessicants" dried up plant leaves; "antitranspirants" coated leaves to reduce water loss. All these were pesticides. Herbicides, the only pesticide at issue in our case, was only one class of chemicals, and though not the smallest, was not the largest category either.

That was just the beginning of my vocabulary morass. There were terms to describe timing. "Pre-emergent" denoted a chemical to be used before plants germinated. "Preplant" meant the pesticide had to be used before the crop went into the ground. "Postemergent" ones had to be used after plants were above ground and had leaves. Sometimes this word applied to the crop and sometimes to the weed, and it made a big difference which.

Application techniques had an elaborate jargon. "Directed" meant to aim the spray at just part of the plant (and know which part).

"Drench" meant soak the soil. "Foliar," soak the leaves. "In-furrow," restrict spraying to just the planting furrow. "Over the top," spray on the growing crop. "Soil incorporate," till in. "Soil application," apply to soil, not vegetation. "Spot treatment," restrict use to small areas.

The language for how the chemicals worked was just as abstract. Contact herbicides killed the plant outright—no subtlety. Translocated herbicides killed first by being absorbed by one part of the plant—stem, roots, or leaves—and then moving throughout the plant. Nonselective agents killed everything. Selective agents killed only certain species and left other plants unharmed.

The chemicals came in a wide variety of forms. "Emulsified concentrations" came in liquids, flowables (or suspended particles), aerosols, and liquified gases. "Dry formulas" included dusts, granules, wettable powders, and soluble powders. Each of these formulas required different spraying equipment and handling methods. For example, wettable powders usually required equipment that would agitate the solution during spraying. Aerosols required "mist-generating" machines.

Intimidating as the herbicide vocabulary was, it was nothing compared to the names of the products. Every chemical had three names—a brand name, a common name, and a chemical name. For example, Treflan, a chemical that in TV ads showed a loving farm dad having time to fish with his kids, was the trade name for trifluralin, which is the common or generic term for 2,6-dinitro-NN-dipropyl-4-trifluoromethylaniline. There were ninety-nine herbicides —all with three colossal names like this—listed in an extension-service weed-control bulletin. This compared with only forty-six "troublesome weeds" listed by the same bulletin. No article or handbook or bulletin I saw ever listed all three names together, so it was impossible to know what chemical I was reading about without consulting charts. And no chart ever gave all three names, either. I always had to consult two charts to learn about one chemical. How did any farmer learn enough to know what he was doing, I wondered. In fact, how did any extension agent or dealer ever get a handle on this, enough to give safe advice?

Still, when I went back to reread some of my favorite scare articles, I had understood enough to notice that most of the agents under attack by environmentalists were insecticides, not herbicides (except for the banned 2,4,5-T). Most of the herbicides in use in Iowa were broken down quickly by microbes into organic compounds such as carbon dioxide, phosphate, or ammonia soon after being sprayed. In addition, some would cling to soil particles until the microbes did their job. That is, they adhered to clay particles so tightly they could not seep through the soil into groundwater or onto roots of nontarget plants. They couldn't drift and cause trouble unless the soil itself was washed or blown away, and even then some would still adhere if the soil dissolved in water.

Some adhered so rapidly it was possible to plant green seedlings within minutes of spraying—as soon as the mist dried. Thus the main hazard in using these types was handling them while the chemical was still active, either concentrated in the container or in spray form in the air. But since most herbicides were low in toxicity to animals, if they were blown by the wind, the risk was to other plants. Goodbye, lilacs, but not cardinals.

In pure form, though, undiluted in the can, most could kill if swallowed and could cause illness if inhaled or in contact with skin. The poison center said most herbicide-accident victims were children who had gotten into improperly stored chemicals. A real pro-herbicidist could argue that household chemicals were more dangerous than farm chemicals. That would be overenthusiastic for my taste, but I was beginning to think that—given reasonable care in handling, and effort to find one that broke down rapidly— the benefits of herbicides might outweigh the dangers. I said so to Mark, who now seemed strangely passive about it.

I noticed too, as I researched, that my attitudes toward chemicals had been formed in the late sixties at the beginning of the environmental movement and that a lot had happened since then. Congress had passed a law in 1972, which took effect in 1976, called the Federal Insecticide, Fungicide, and Rodenticide Act. The act went by the puppylike name FIFRA and in essence required that all pesticides be registered with the Environmental Protection Agency. The EPA then classified chemicals for either general or restricted use.

Restricted-use chemicals could only be handled by a certified user, someone who had passed an exam on proper application and disposal. (Much of what I learned came from studying manuals for these licensing exams.) As for "general use," these were chemicals that "harmed the applicator or the environment very little or not at all when used exactly as directed on the label." The EPA spelled out in great regulatory detail what those labels must contain. They must give brand and common names, a list of active ingredients, a description of hazards to people, animals, and environment, and instructions on how to prevent those hazards through proper handling. For example, when using a chemical labeled toxic to bees, the user had to notify beekeepers within two miles at least twenty-four hours in advance. The label had to define what pests the chemical controlled, what crops it could be used on, how and in what form it could be applied, how much to use, where to use it, and when. Just as important, the label had to have a "misuse statement" of when not to use it and how to store and dispose of containers properly.

I was reassured by all this. Maybe herbicides were a "less bad" class of chemicals, and maybe I could trust the government to keep the really bad stuff out of the hands of untrained people. So in trusting mind I ventured to read the label of a "general use" herbicide. True, it was not one of the ones the forester was recommending, but it was classified "general use": A "highly active herbicide which can move with the surface runoff water, can remain phytotoxic for a year or more. . ."

Phytotoxic? What was a word like that doing on a label for laymen? To the dictionary: "poisonous to plants." Back to the label: "Do not contaminate cropland, water, or irrigation ditches. Do not apply in the vicinity of sensitive crops. Do not store near other pesticides." And on and on it went, saying this stuff should never come in contact with soil or water or else. If this were for general use, I thought, what in hell was scary enough to be restricted? I went back to reread the definition of general use and saw again the phrase "when used exactly"—that was the key word, *exactly*—"as directed on the label." I thought of a neighbor we liked, a fellow who claimed to be only one of two organic farmers in the country, who kept two beehives sitting in his front yard. Those hives had charmed us and we stopped one day to meet the fellow.

"They're empty," he told us. "Damn neighbor sprayed without telling me and I didn't have a chance to cover my bees. Killed them all. Keep the hives there so I don't forget I'm mad."

I thought also of the time we were forced indoors because one farmer insisted on spraying on a windy day. Almost all those "exact" labels say don't spray in the wind. Thinking of this I really understood the issue for the first time. Who on earth is exact?

But even this insight seemed glib on reflection. To blame careless users was too simple. For example, according to EPA regulation, a label must define toxicity to humans precisely, and these are the words that, by law, must be used: "Danger" means highly toxic; a taste to a teaspoonful can kill a person. "Warning" means moderately toxic; it takes a teaspoonful to two tablespoons to kill you. "Caution" means low toxicity; you'd have to swallow an ounce to a pint to be dispatched. I asked a friend of mine, a farmer's wife, what the words "danger," "warning," and "caution" meant to her.

"They mean 'be careful,'" she said.

"Did you know on labels they have different meanings?" I asked.

When she said no, we spent a few minutes walking through their shed inspecting labels. Not very scientific research, but it confirmed my feeling that not all the laws in the world could protect us from ourselves. It's not easy to be careful in a complex world. Who on earth knows enough to be exact?

In the end I recommended we use a post-emergent, translocated herbicide in liquid emulsion, applied in foliar spot treatments by backpack sprayer. It worked beautifully. I was uncomfortable with the decision, but I felt we had been reasonable and careful. I thought Mark felt the same. He didn't protest and he did most of the spraying. What I failed to see was that perhaps he had accepted herbicides, but he could not accept that it was a living myth who told us to use them.

STONE

CHAPTER EIGHT

STONE

Mark gave me a set of wind chimes tuned, said the brochure, to an ancient Grecian scale. Whatever their heritage, their clamor—a melody, not a clink—was unceasing pleasure for me. I hung them on the front porch. I had tried to tell Mark when we first met that it wasn't my name but the sound of it I cared about. Sounds mattered to me. I wanted only the lyric of my name, not its meaning, from him. But I am clumsy about explaining distinctions like that. Then he gave me this gift of sound, a perfect reflection of my sense of the place. I thought he understood.

Even now, whenever I think of the farm, I think of its sounds, because sound was the easiest of the senses for me. I always heard the seasons before I saw them. In spring, long after everyone else would be seeing robins, when robins were marching in six-column platoons on county roads, I'd still not have seen any. But I'd be the first to hear the frogs begin their bellowing, sounding to me as if there were more frogs on our one pond than stars above.

The sound of a whippoorwill would invariably follow the frogs a few nights later, and I'd be the first to hear that too, its single call somehow more strident than the noise of the frog millions. It always sounded surprised, as if indignant for being made to call at night, a rare occurrence among birds. I had not heard whippoorwills before my first spring on the farm, but I knew the sound anyway. Whippoorwills sounded exactly as I imagined they should.

Decoding sounds was a shared challenge for us, both city kids— Mark the New Yorker, me the Chicagoan. Our training taught us to distinguish bus from dump truck, not oriole from goldfinch. We learned wild sounds by freezing in place in woods or pasture, hoping for a glimpse of the bird or animal that made the noise. More easily we mastered farm sounds, such as the cry of a sheep separated from the flock—it infuriated me how the flock never answered the lost one—or the grumbling of hogs being loaded into trucks for the one-way trip to market. One sound defied our decoding for a long time. It was a sound cattle made, a roar of rage or pain, but always from one animal at a time. Then Bird, one of our goats, kidded for the first time. Her bellows were different, but even so the connection was clear. How could we not have realized we were hearing cows calving?

I heard more than I ever saw. Seeing was difficult for me. Outside my study window, on any given afternoon, I might see a cat perched on a fencepost, or our three goats arrayed on a hillside, or a lumpy pile of debris left from a spring storm, or several wild ducks floating or diving on the pond, or our weed garden with an occasional flower or vegetable for competition, or, above the woods to the north horizon, perhaps a small thunderstorm bathed pink in a sunset, its band of rain a sliver beneath the cloud, catching the light also. All that could change in a moment. The cat would launch herself after a mouse; the goats move to another hill; the storm shift, perhaps moving closer. The changes in plants, animals, and weather were too rapid to see. Once I noticed a blue heron in the swamp just over our north fence. It stayed for days, preening itself and watching us watch it. Once I saw a flicker on the pond, focused on it, saw it was only the shadow of a dog and saw before I lost focus that the dog was a coyote. In the dusk I could not see the coyote itself, only the reflection. Glimpses like that were rare.

The day we planted our trees, our small army of friends helping us, we were noisy at first, but as the rhythm of the work took hold, each of us fell silent. As I sank my shovel, rocked it, slipped in a seedling, and closed the slit, over and over, the rhythm set my thoughts wandering for a time. Then the rhythm emptied my mind entirely. There was only the work of it, so simple, but over and over and over. Then in the rhythm I began *seeing* the ground: ferns curled in whorls, wildflowers emerging, tiny May apples, miniature goldenrod, tiny Virginia creeper—hundreds of things I usually was able to see only when they were large and unavoidably evident.

If I stopped work to look, the ground became invisible again, still late winter brown. But if I kept the rhythm going I saw unemerged things in their April beginnings. This was our woods; we owned it, walked it, cut firewood from it, made payments on it, fixed fences around it—how little I saw of it. That night neither aspirin nor brandy relieved the soreness I felt from planting, but neither would the soreness cloud the pleasant clarity planting our woods had brought me.

Touch, though not so accessible as sound, was far easier than sight for me. Things touched never changed their feel: rock, warm and heavy as I moved it in place around flower beds; weeds as they finally yielded to a tug; mud sucking at my feet when I stepped in the pond for a swim; grass wet on my ankles in the morning when I went to the barn to milk the goats; the goats themselves, silky in contrast to the coarse fuzziness of sheep; the odd tickle of kids nibbling a sleeve.

When Bird's kids were born I sat in the pen with her, holding her, anxious not to miss a moment. When I was sure she was in labor—pawing the ground and bleating—I ran to the house—running because I was afraid in the two minutes I'd be gone, she'd deliver. I got rags and hot water, as the book had told me; iodine and nursing bottles, as my neighbor had told me; and I tried to clip my nails, as the vet had told me, in case I had to "help." Heaven help poor Bird if I did; my hand was shaking so, I nearly cut my fingers instead. The barn cat joined us in the pen; she and Bird were constant companions. All of a sudden the cat began writhing and twisting in the hay. I leaned over to see what was bothering her and saw she too was giving birth—to four kittens.

Two hours later Bird was in heavy labor, lying down, bellowing. The sac began to appear and I could see inside it the tips of the kid's feet and nose. I reached out to touch it and the creature, startled, withdrew from my hand. I was stunned. I hadn't imagined it could respond, that a creature half-born could feel and react to touch.

Taste, the coarsest, least lyrical of the senses, had lured us toward this lifestyle to begin with—even while we were still in Tennessee. We had rented a house there, a nice house, but to me no better than any other I'd lived in growing up in Chicago suburbs. To Mark, though, it was a wonder. He had never lived in a house. He would walk from room to room, amazed that windows occurred on all four sides and looked upon space, not on alleys or shafts. A door led outside, not into a hall, and there was more than one. He would walk out one door and come in another just for the wonder of it: front door, side porch door, back porch door, a pair of French doors leading to the strangest phenomenon of all—our garden.

This Tennessee garden, our first, was a scraggly one, but nothing in Mark's experience had prepared him for it. His mother couldn't be bothered to keep even a cactus, so all of it was utterly new to him: the feel of the soil, its color, its smell; the unfolding leaves, the shapes of seeds. Seeds intimidated him. If the envelope said plant a quarter-inch deep, he felt that meant as measured by ruler. I told him seeds had been evolving for millions of years and were glad enough to touch dirt. He wasn't convinced. He measured.

He read anything he could find; ransacked the libraries and extension office; buttonholed neighbors and friends for advice; and hounded me with questions about things I'd never thought about. Soil tilth. Mulching. Organic pest control. Companion planting. My parents had gardened, but they were from the put-it-in-the-ground-and-see-if-it-grows school. Mark made me be more serious. He didn't want seeds out the door; he wanted an accomplishment. The more he experienced, the more he wanted. When the leaf lettuce was ready, he marveled at the different colors, tastes, and crispnesses and decided he wanted no more store lettuce—which set him dreaming of a greenhouse. When he tasted young carrots, he wanted a root cellar. When we shared the first tomato—we had watched it ripen for days; I wouldn't let him pick it too early—he wanted us to grow enough to can our own winter sauces.

Then came the corn. The wait for it had been eternal. The silks had to be brown and the ears look full, I'd told him. One evening we checked and I said they were ready; he reached to pick one.

"Not yet," I said. "First we put water on to boil."

"What?" he said.

When the water was boiling, I ran to the corn patch; he walked behind me. I tore off several ears and frantically shucked them. Mark was moving too slowly.

"Hurry," I said. "It's important to move as fast as you can."

I ran toward the kitchen. He didn't, so I yelled to him, "I'm serious. *Run*. You must run."

He was puzzled, but he ran. Into the boiling pot, wait five minutes, no more, and hand him an ear; no plates, no table. I'd looked forward to this for months. The sugar in corn kernels is short-lived, at its peak only at ripening; the instant an ear is picked, the sugar begins to change to starch. Ear corn from the supermarket, picked last week, is acceptable; ear corn from a roadside stand, picked that morning, is excellent. But nothing can compare with garden corn eaten minutes after picking while the sugar is intact. Gardeners wait all year for this secret moment; other people never suspect it's possible. Mark laughed, he was so pleased; he wandered to and fro in the kitchen, tasting, exclaiming, tasting again. At the window he paused to look at the garden. "We will always live in a house," he said. "We will always have a garden."

I like to remember him that way, running for the corn. I thought from so many moments like it that hearing, seeing, tasting, the sense—or senses—of the place, were the experiences we shared. Senses, these were the quests. I thought farm life was to be an examination of these things; the real farm, like the kaleidoscope of feathers, was whatever we managed to perceive. And perception was difficult. The first thing we had talked about, on our rock so many years ago, was perception. But now with several gardens behind us, I was beginning to wonder. What did he perceive here? Did he hear the whippoorwills?

I was alone in the house one particular day, a Saturday. The forester had shown up so early that morning that we weren't even up, which, since we were always up early to milk the goats, was incredibly early. He wanted Mark to go with him because he'd finally found a collapsing barn with a stone foundation which the owner would let him salvage for his hearth. Mark left with him right away because he wanted stone to put around the deep beds he'd been digging in the garden. It was all a blur of activity, so I wasn't sure what they were up to, except that they'd just given me some time alone with the place—what was left of it.

I sat down at my desk, still in my bathrobe, still nursing my first cup of coffee, and looked out my window, that wonderful window. Normally the view was my anchor, but this particular Saturday, as it had been for many mornings, it was a distressing riot of trenches. Mark was digging deep beds in the garden.

The beds had been yet another of the forester's ideas. This gardening method was supposed to coax large yields from small spaces. The principle was simple. Dig very deeply, then never step on the dug beds. The loose soil allowed roots to grow downwards rather than sideways. Plants could then be crammed together. As they became larger, their leaves would shade the ground, letting fewer weeds grow and reducing water evaporation. This should have meant less weeding and watering, a notion that especially appealed to Mark. He interpreted less to mean none.

I was skeptical of that part, but that was not my reason for resisting the idea. I couldn't see why we needed deep beds. The method suited people who had little space for a garden and no machinery. There was only a small patch of cleared ground in front of the forester's house and he owned no tiller. So deep beds made sense for him. We had acres of fields and a fine tiller. Why bother? Still, if Mark wanted to dig, I reasoned, let him.

The usual method of digging a bed, called "bastard trenching," was to remove a fork-depth strip of soil and place it in a wheelbarrow. The soil under that was disturbed—not dug—by waggling a fork. Topsoil from the neighboring strip was then put over the first. This technique loosened soil to about twenty inches. The bastard trencher then was to continue working strips, using soil in the wheelbarrow to top off the last strip. I've done bastard trenching. It's easy; it takes me about two hours for a ten-foot bed.

Mark, however, interpreted bastard to mean lazy. To him, laziness was expediency; expediency was compromise; compromise was lack of commitment; and lack of commitment was betrayal. So he decided he would have to take three feet of soil completely out of each bed and mix the layers in order to be morally correct. I told him I didn't think soil should be disturbed so much. He said roots can grow down to a depth of three feet, so three feet the beds would be dug. There was clay under there, I said. He'd mix it with cow manure, he said, and put me to work digging about a generation's worth of manure out of the barn. He created a splendid disorder beneath the window, until finally the forester noticed what he was doing.

Soil was a fragile ecosystem, the forester said. Disturbing layers so deeply could wreck the micro-organic communities within it. In fact, it could be years before the soil recovered from the digging Mark had already done. The forester told Mark this as gently as possible, perhaps too gently, because Mark kept digging, but now the idea fueling his effort was that digging deeply would mean the beds would never have to be redug. They would be loosened forever.

I had to return some tools to the forester one afternoon and found him digging in his own beds. He'd just invented a special fork that would loosen a full twenty inches with one waggle, and he was quite pleased with himself. "But do you have to redig the beds every year?"

"Of course," he said.

Mark finally stopped at twenty-six inches—six inches deeper than the bastard method, true, but ten inches shy of his goal. He'd dug some admirable holes. They awed me, but troubled me too. I was afraid they'd never be refilled because Mark seemed too discouraged. He saw those holes as a failure, a compromise, a self-betrayal.

I studied the mounds from my window and considered the digger. What was happening to him? Where was reason? Why did he think doing something the hard way was the better commitment? Why was compromise so dreadful for him? The beds seemed mad to me, an excess of effort compounded by error. Most bewildering of all was that he now seemed to blame the forester for his own confusion. And his anger was in terms of trust. He felt betrayed.

My thoughts were troubling me. I left the window and picked my way through the house. The wood floors, like the view out the window, were normally an anchor for me. Sometimes when my work palled, I'd stop and patrol the house, reconnect with the reality of the floors, always overbright with window light, before returning to the unreality of whatever article or lecture I was working on. At that moment, though, the floors were covered with sheets of plastic and heaped with debris and paraphernalia. Every room in the house had been disturbed by our wood stove installation. Sections of steel chimney littered my study floor. The kitchen was full of tools and chemicals; the living room coated with plaster dust and piles of laths. We were tearing out a wall between the living and dining rooms to make space for the stove.

The project was a nightmare. Every misuse of tool imaginable, every mispurchase of materials possible—we did it. Things had been tense in our house. Part of the tension was my feeling that we weren't being practical. I was sure the carpentry was so far beyond our skills that, like the deep beds in the garden, we'd never finish. Where was reason?

A strange outburst from the forester a few days before began to make sense to me. He had stopped by to check on our progress with the installation and made a suggestion, a good one. I'd complimented him on how much he knew.

"Do I? Do I?" he'd said, his voice tense. "I only wish I knew as much as people think I do."

I was shocked by his tone. Who had been angry with him recently to make him so defensive? Despite his rhetoric—"love nature, save wildlife"—I had come to think of him as a scientist, not a living myth. My perception had changed. I thought of him as curious, more interested in knowledge than philosophy, even if what he learned warred with his values. If facts conflicted with his ideals, his choice was simple: compromise the ideal. He wasn't looking for something to believe in.

Other people were, though. Other people wanted a vision to pursue—ideal farms, not real ones. To them the forester would be a source not of information but of truth. Was that what had happened? Had someone believed in him too much? The forester must have a great deal of confusion about him, I thought. He had information to give, but most people wanted myths. If the people he tried to help wanted to be living myths, then he was doomed to betray them. He would, being reasonable, ask them to compromise. And that—as I watched Mark dig his beds—was one thing a living myth cannot do. To compromise was to question the ideal, reinvent perception, lose faith. I was beginning to think that where I saw cats and coyotes, Mark saw compromise and the death of his dream. I was dreading the stone's arrival. It would be just one more ideal to cope with.

Eventually a strange truck pulled up, hauling a huge flatbed trailer piled with stone. Mark jumped out, introduced the driver, Hoss; his wife, Janet; and their two-year-old son, Jake. The five of us began pulling stone off the truck, Jake too, his baby efforts to help making us laugh. The stone was heaped into a messy but at least invisible pile behind the shed. Mark seemed upset, so I talked to Hoss. He was a logger, made his living by cutting and selling firewood. He was sensitive, I discovered at once—the hard way. I asked him what his real name was. I assumed Hoss was a nickname he'd picked up because of his size. The question hurt his feelings. Hoss was his real name.

"What's the matter?" I asked Mark when they had left.

"I'd never realized what a lazy guy the forester is before."

Lazy equaling expedient equaling betrayal? "How so?" I asked.

"I worked hard to help him pick out his stone; he kept telling me, 'work smarter, not harder,' but he spent a lot of time picking out the best stone for himself. It came time to pick my stone, he picked junk and kept taking breaks. I'd tell him, 'Is that what you mean by work smarter?'"

It sounded to me that the forester had been reasonable. He was picking stone for a hearth, not a garden, so he should have been careful. As for taking breaks, people should pace themselves when doing physical work.

"Is that all that happened?" I said.

"No." He thought a minute, trying to decide how to explain. "I asked Hoss if he knew anyone who was selling a small tractor. Hoss said his was for sale, an Allis Chalmers, a real antique, 1941. So we were talking and I was getting interested and the forester jumps into the conversation and says he wants to buy it."

"Did you say you were definitely interested?" I asked.

"No, but I obviously was, and he jumps right into a deal like that."

The ultimate betrayal, of course. Mark was trying to be coolly interested — to keep the price down — and his friend becomes a bidding rival.

It wouldn't have been enough for me to end a friendship, but it was for Mark, and I was sorry. I liked the forester. He had never asked me to believe anything he told me. I'd miss that. But for Mark the tractor war had been the last peg in a growing distrust that had begun with the herbicides. Mark's decision, I realized, would baffle the forester. To a pragmatist, a friendship is like a fact; if it conflicts with a philosophy, the choice is simple: compromise the ideal. To a living myth, if a friendship conflicts with an ideal, the choice is simple: the friend has to go. Neither would understand the other's choice.

Though I was sorry to lose the forester, I was relieved too. I thought now there'd be less pressure on me from Mark. His enthusiasm for project after project was wearing me out. The forester never suggested we do any of those things. He just told us about geese, deep beds, wood stoves, tree farming, solar heat. Mark would take it from there and insist we try them. I was drowning. Projects were taking too much of my time; my work was suffering; we'd spent too much money; the house was a mess. . . .

That night Mark asked me when I'd start the research for the solar-heat project. I sat stone silent. Weeks before the forester had said we could get up to a third of our heat from solar energy if we converted the front porch to a greenhouse. The inevitable sketches on graph paper followed. It did sound interesting. We could make panels from tin and set up a flow of air through them that would certainly heat the upstairs bedrooms. But we'd have to think of some way to insulate the greenhouse at night. All of this required time, money, and skills. We were short on all three. I wanted to wait a year or two until other projects were done. With Mark angry at the forester, surely he'd forget the solar project. But no. He looked more determined than ever to begin.

I started to protest. Time, money, skills. But I stopped. At long last I was grasping that none of these were at issue. Our arguments had never been about cisterns and deep beds. The issue all along had been perception. He wanted to see the farm as a living ideal. I wanted to see it, period. I wanted to struggle to understand the view out my window. He wanted to struggle to change it.

He wanted to be a living myth.

And I didn't.

I couldn't.

Time. Money. Skills.

Suddenly I envied the Asheville couple. I had laughed when I'd heard they'd abandoned their dream life in the country and were now living in town. He drove from drugstore to drugstore, setting up displays of sunglasses. He now seemed less silly than we, who had torn house and fields to pieces. What I really envied was whatever had given them the courage to turn against their dream instead of each other. How strong was Mark's need for an ideal? He had just easily chosen it over a friendship. Could he compromise if the choice were between it and a wife?

Mark repeated his question again, more gently. I had promised, he said, to do the solar research. He was puzzled by my silence. It wasn't like me to be so quiet. "You aren't going to do it, are you?" he said finally. Still I was silent. The creak of the windmill filled the quiet. Time. Money. Skills. Reality.

"Patty?" Mark asked. He sounded frightened. Was he, too, seeing the future? The night was filled with the usual night sounds—the frogs, the whippoorwills, the wind chimes. And owls *whooing* on the roof.

BLUE CLAY

CHAPTER NINE

BLUE CLAY

The well lasted five years.

In fact, it outlasted Mark and me. We had been divorced for two years when it failed. Wieland had long since retired. One morning, as the windmill spun, the shaft began racking and heaving so roughly that even though I'd never heard such a sound before, I knew. I watched it rattle a moment, then walked to the cistern to listen for the familiar splash. The cistern was silent—and nearly empty.

After countless phone calls I found another wellman, Steve Rich of Kalona. Steve changed the leathers on the pump to restore the vacuum in the pipe and water began pumping again. But he said the well was in bad shape; all the pipes had corroded and the screen— the filter that water passed through into the pipe—was virtually clogged. If it failed again, there was nothing more he could do. I would have to drill. Unlike the wellman five years earlier, Steve seemed genuinely sorry, as if he'd told me a favorite dog would have to be put to sleep. And that's exactly how it felt. Three weeks later, on a Sunday, the well failed again. On Monday I went to the bank and borrowed $3,000. On Tuesday Steve showed up in his pickup.

Behind him were two monster trucks, one a tanker carrying two thousand gallons of water—to cool and lubricate the drill. The drill was on the second truck; I watched, amazed, as the rig uncoiled from that truck and rose to over forty feet, higher than my windmill.

Besides Steve, there were two rig operators. One worked the left side of the truck; the other, the right. The one on the right spent the entire day shoveling all the debris and water the drill pulled up out of a catch basin and onto my lawn. It was pitiless, unceasing, backbreaking labor. Never mind what it did to the lawn. The operator on the left, however, stood the whole day with a hand on the drill shaft. That was it. He never moved or spoke, except occasionally to call Steve over to inspect something.

Steve and I, meanwhile, sat on the porch all day and talked. I teased about the lazy worker on the left. Steve said, no, I had it wrong. The guy on the left had the skill; he was feeling the soil layers. He could tell by the slightest change in vibration what the drill was working through. Because layers change so quickly, he had to keep his hand constantly on the shaft. It took lots of concentration to drill.

"How does he learn all that?" I asked.

"See the guy on the right?" Steve said. "After about five years of breaking his back like that, maybe he'll get promoted, but not many guys last long enough to move over to the other side of the truck."

Steve had done that, worked his five years on the right, then finally, several years on the left, and now he was promoted to sitting on the porch chatting. His skills would be demonstrated the next day when he installed the electrical mechanism, dug a line into the house, and rigged up a jet pump for pressure in the house pipes. Today, though, there wasn't much for him to do except talk geology with me—and make decisions.

The key matter to be decided was, had they dug deeply enough? Just hitting water was not the goal. In fact, they probably started hitting water at about forty or fifty feet, he said. "What we're looking for is *pure* water and that will have to be below blue clay. The clay coming up now is all yellow. See the color?"

It was definitely yellow. Blue clay was a better pollution barrier than other soil types, he said. It took fifty years for a drop of water to penetrate a layer of blue clay, so odds were the water beneath it was safe. This was the first I'd grasped that well failure was not due to lack of water, at least not here.

"How long will my new well last?" I asked.

"Maybe forever," Rich said. "Wells used to fail every ten or fifteen years—the screens would corrode or silt up. But in the last ten years there have been incredible advances in materials and technology.

We're putting six-inch plastic pipe in—theoretically it could outlast the ground around it. How long did your old well last?"

"I think fifty-seven years, as best as I can tell from the abstracts."

"That's pretty good, but these new wells are all made of plastics. They'll never corrode."

My mind began spinning. If the well could last forever, could I put the windmill over it? I had been assuming all these years that I would have to give up my windmill when the well failed. "If I moved my windmill over this new well, I wouldn't have to redrill again in a few years, right?"

Steve thought so. I started seriously thinking about the idea. It had only been a few days since the well failed, but already I missed the windmill. The house didn't feel right without its flickering shadow outside or its soft clacketing as the shaft rose and fell. I couldn't bear the thought of it useless, just there. Part of the magic had been that it worked, it pumped a well. If I moved it, I'd have a new, modern, all-plastic well pumped by an old-fashioned windmill. "You think I could hook up the well to my old cistern?" I asked.

"Sure."

"You think I'm crazy for even thinking of such a thing, don't you?"

Steve said he'd grown up around windmills; he knew how special they were; he wanted to get one for his own farm sort of as an advertisement for his well company. In fact, he was hoping I'd want to sell him mine. No, he really understood how I felt. But a banker or realtor or a future buyer might not, he warned.

There he'd done it, brought up the real question in all this. Did I plan to sell or keep the place? Leave or stay?

Family and friends alike had been stunned by my decision to keep the farm after the divorce. How could such a practical, reasonable person lose touch with reality? they worried. Even I had trouble explaining the decision. I thought it was, at least in part, my pragmatism that drove Mark and me apart. Actually I didn't fully understand what had happened; perhaps I never would. But I did know I had begun to look more and more expedient to him as months went by. To him I was becoming the sort of person who would sacrifice an ideal because it wasn't practical. Such an expedient person wouldn't keep at farming by herself, would she? Wasn't I too sensible to be so foolish? My family wondered.

But two years had gone by and still I stayed. "The place is killing you," my brother would say almost every time he saw me.

I had taken two jobs to keep up payments. I'd sold the goats because I couldn't take care of them and work full-time too. I'd kept the chickens and geese, but I had not planted any new trees or had a garden since the separation. I did make a list of things that I wanted to do with the place and hung it in the kitchen. The list was four feet long. And untouched. My sister told me once that after any visit, the conversation in the car the first few miles from the farm was always about that list. How did she stand it? Why did she abuse herself this way? When would she come to her senses and sell the place? Keeping the farm was too tough, too expensive for one person, and a woman at that. This was obvious to them; why not to me?

Well, actually, it was obvious to me. I stayed at first, I told myself, just to rest from the stormy year preceding our divorce. It had been chaotic, baffling, and painful waiting for and trying to prevent it. But two years of this I knew was inertia, not rest. I had become so busy trying to survive that I'd not even hiked the hills. What was the point of living in such a place if I had no way to enjoy it?

So then I began telling myself that I kept at it because I'd hoped the problem was temporary, that I would figure out a way to support myself and the farm too. But was this fantasy? Was a future hope worth *years* of stress? Why did I want a farm in the first place? Friends would ask that question and I had no good answer. Why did I stay? I had a friend in town I was avoiding because every time I talked to him he tried to tell me my stubborn attempt to keep living in the country was destroying me. I avoided him because I was afraid I might start to agree with him. And I did want to stay, didn't I?

I had been coping with my dilemma by avoiding it. As the drill spun, though, I at last yielded to the reality that I couldn't avoid much longer. I would have to choose rather than just survive. If I were going to stay, I'd have to have chosen to stay—and have a good reason for it.

Leave? Then I should make things as conventional as possible. Modern homebuyers want their water automatic. No fooling with turning on a windmill, no cleaning out cisterns. Rehooking the windmill would cut the value of the property. If I were leaving, I should sell the windmill to Steve.

Stay? Then why should I care if my tastes hurt the book value of the place? If I were staying I should have Steve move the windmill over the new well. Sell it or move it? Leave or stay?

"Blue clay!" The left-hand rig man waved energetically at Steve. Then I saw it, slime-blue ooze washing out of the pipe, getting bluer as the drill spun.

"Now we're looking for coarse sand," Steve explained. The screen needed to be set in rocky sand; that was the most likely soil in this area to have a fast enough flow to supply a house and farm. Fine sand would be too slow and could clog the screen; clay or most stone would not let water flow. The ideal would be to find porous stone because it would not clog or shift. But stone layers like that were rare in this glacial-till region.

After a few minutes, sand began spilling into the basin. Steve and the drillman conferred. Too fine. Down a little more. I shuddered at that decision because every inch down was another dollar. Finally after what felt like hundreds of dollars, the coarse sand appeared, the drilling stopped, and the two rigmen began to sink the plastic pipe into the hole. As they were setting the final section, Steve turned and hollered, "Windmill or electric?" I stood there.

"Which? I've got to know now," Steve said. All three were looking at me. Leave-electric? Or stay-windmill?

"Electric," I said, then added, "But I can't sell you the windmill. Not yet. Not now."

Vines grew up on the windmill. Occasionally I'd turn it on to amuse guests, and when I did, I'd check the cistern, still hoping for a splash. Two realtors and a banker told me to tear it down. But I couldn't, not until I knew if I were staying—and why.

BARRY'S SUMMER

CHAPTER TEN

BARRY'S SUMMER

Barry's summer—odd how I've come to think of it as *his* summer—was a nightmare from beginning to end. This, the first after drilling the new well, started with cold rains, ideal for poison ivy, which grew with unprecedented lushness, spreading from the fields toward the house, over fences, through flower beds, until every step outside became a risk. Heat and drought, the worst since the 1930s, followed the cold. Headlines described devastated corn yields and dying livestock. I endured insects.

Insects loved the 110-degree heat. They thrived, bullied, attacked the porch, the kitchen, the bedroom, the bed. I patted caulking cord around the screens, but creatures unknown to my guidebooks crawled through anyway—beetles small as fleas, lime-green hoppers smaller than pepper specks, and able to bite.

I dreaded the nights. Moths clustered on the door waiting for my puppy to bark. When I'd open the door for her, in they'd swarm, filling the kitchen with a malevolent flickering, reminding me why the legend began that moths are the souls of the damned. It was better to turn off the lights and hide from all of them. I watched a lot of television in the dark that summer, through an insect-coated screen.

In past, less evil, summers, cicadas merely hummed in the trees. This summer, though, they attacked the house, at each landing shrieking like banshees. They even resembled goblins as they hugged the screen, their white underbellies and oversize transparent wings veined with what looked like lead. If moths were the dead, cicadas were the demons that tormented them. The puppy found them great toys; she delighted in catching them, unaware of me inside, cringing at every crunch of her teeth against those cicadian hulls.

Once disgust with her overcame my revulsion, and I stood on the porch swatting them away from her. I had to give up—too many; let her chew. As I retreated inside I felt something on my shoulder, brushed it, and dislodged a cicada riding there. It screamed, diving and rediving for my head until I knocked it senseless against a wall. Dead, I thought, but covered it with a towel to be sure. I could not bring myself to touch it. At dawn I was awakened by a cicada's scream and watched with horror from my bed as the towel heaved in the hall. A bad summer. A nightmare. An assault.

Up on the foundation ledge I saw some torn corrugated cardboard. I walked toward it, vaguely irritated, thinking uncharitably, why couldn't college students at least manage to clean out a basement right? And then—it was barely a thought, but enough to make me pause before touching it—I didn't ever remember any trash up there, and looked again. A slow deep chill crept through me as the cardboard resolved itself into a snake.

One night I noticed a light on in the basement and assumed the two students I'd hired to do odd jobs for me had left it on; they'd been patching cracks that morning. I went down to turn it off and took a moment to study the walls. Besides the tangled threads of cracks, there were broad swatches where coarse gravel fill was exposed. My walls looked like a painting, an intricate gray image that absorbed me for many minutes. I found in the aesthetics an excuse not to return to the insects and heat upstairs.

Awareness and horror rushed over me in equal measure as I saw clearly first the black and yellow markings unevenly spaced, then the tail which lay curled in a crevice and so pointed out the hole above the window it had crawled through. Then the eyes. Its pupils were large and round and awake and seeing me. We locked eyes. Then full horror sank in. I saw that the snake, stretched rod straight on the ledge, completely filled it from window to hall. I had measured that wall recently; it was four feet eleven inches. The tail off the ledge was about another four inches. This snake was big.

I could not move.

I remember this moment as one where fear had chased reason so far away, reason could not regain control. Reason was saying distantly, Just shut the door and leave the room. Reason was arguing that a snake in the basement is no different from any home maintenance problem. First you analyze it; then you solve it—or ignore it. But I could not move. Horror was much stronger than sense, and completely in control, holding me in a real moment with a dream paralysis. It seemed a long time, though perhaps it was brief as a dream, before reason did return and I shut the door and went upstairs, sensibly turning out the light first. After all, that was what I'd come down for.

Leaving the basement offered no comfort. I was upset—unreasonably so. I went to my reptile guidebook, one I seldom use because I don't like looking at pictures of snakes. I already knew by the coloring—and by reason—that it wasn't poisonous. A bull snake, the book told me.

The bull snake, *Pituophis melanoleucus sayi*, is a large heavy snake, active in the day, a constrictor averaging five feet but often reaching seven, the book told me. It is yellowish, usually with forty-one or more black or brown body blotches—I marveled that some people care to count such things. There were other details: pointed snout, internasal scales, four prefrontal scales, scales keeled in twenty-seven to thirty-seven rows. None of this made any sense to me. What did make sense was an odd sermon accompanying the description: "All bull snakes should be protected against wanton killing. There is no doubt of their value as one agent in rodent control."

I had been plagued by pocket gophers that spring. Conditions ideal for poison ivy had been just as favorable for gophers. They ravaged my asparagus, fruit trees, and Russian olives. Then suddenly the gophers had disappeared. The asparagus rallied. Over the summer I'd also had construction in and about the house, so piles of debris had accumulated in the yard. I'd been worried about attracting rats but had seen none. I was thinking the explanation was stretched that moment beneath my feet. I'd lived on this farm long enough to know that any change in the animal-pest population usually meant a predator had moved in. But I hadn't thought of a snake.

The guidebook concluded its sermon by noting that bull snakes made excellent pets. This I could not imagine for me. In fact, I was having difficulty simply forcing myself to sit in the chair in my living room, which was directly above the ledge in the basement, and I felt somehow that snake might penetrate the floor. I eyed the heating grates. Reason argued that even if the snake managed to tear open the furnace-room door, unlatch the firebox, climb in, deduce the pipe route to my chair, and peer at me through the grate, still, big as that animal was, it could not get through the openings. Reason lost. I fled the chair.

As I wrestled with my feelings I became aware of how extreme they were. By then I'd lived in the country for half a decade and coped with things other folks find overwhelming: skunks under the porch, birds in the attic, muskrats in the pond, ticks, slugs, thistles, nettles, barn rats, raccoons. I'd sat in that same chair one night while a raccoon raided a bird's nest and watched the drama with calm fascination. Only later did it occur to me that town people would have rushed out with misguided altruism to save the bird. Conditioned to country life, I automatically assumed a raccoon had as much right to a bird as a bird had to a bug. But put a snake in my basement and this tough country mind became dithery as a schoolgirl's, the kind whose talent for screaming inspires boys to put toads in her lunchbag. Why was I suddenly like that? I had a shotgun; I knew how to use it. All I had to do was walk down there and blast that animal; that would solve the problem.

But I was remembering things. Two years ago I returned from the barn after milking the goats and saw a small bull snake on the kitchen porch. I poked it with a hoe and it fled. The same snake? I'd seen snakeskins behind the garage several times. Were they progressively larger each time? Could they belong to the same snake? More compelling was the vermin I didn't see. This snake lived here. It was policing the place. It was a benefactor, a protector.

Reason was thus becoming determined the snake would live. Emotion recoiled, though, as I imagined the obvious consequence.

If I wanted that snake alive, I might have to catch it. No. At least, no, not tonight. At least, no, preferably not ever. Emotion was so overwrought that not only was touching it out of the question, but sleeping tonight with it loose in the house was looking more and more unlikely.

Reason then suggested simply that I name the snake.

A name occurred to me immediately—Baryshnikov. The dancer reminded me of strength and grace; and so did the snake. So Baryshnikov it would be. Barry for short, of course. I tried the name out a few times: "Well, Barry, I wish you weren't where you are." That helped. "Barry, you need to know the house rules. Rule one: Don't eat the puppy." Yes, speaking aloud helped. "Pleasant dreams, Barry. You, no doubt, will dream of gophers. I will probably dream of you."

I did sleep that night, fitfully, and of course I dreamed of snakes. In the dream I remember most clearly, it was day and I stood on the second floor of the house dressed in shorts and a T-shirt. I could not see the snake, but somehow I knew it was now twelve feet long. It was in the living room, thrashing about from one end of the room to the other in a sideways figure-eight pattern. I also knew the snake would not come upstairs, but neither could I go down to see it. I awoke then and recognized the thrashing sound in my dream as the puppy tossing a toy about on the porch. And it really was day. The dream had left me with a peaceful feeling. This was slowly replaced by dread as I remembered it wasn't entirely a dream.

My returning discomfort was accompanied by a new feeling: puzzlement. I was in no danger at all. Why this horror and dread? And why so extreme? My reactions bordered on phobic. The reluctance to touch it, the dread of snake photos—these were behaviors psychologists looked for when they needed subjects for phobia research. Yet I didn't feel like a phobic. My reaction to the cicada—now that was phobic. But this felt different. The source of my fear wasn't entirely with *me*, it seemed. Puzzle or no, I did have a real snake to deal with. I decided to stall reality by thinking about the dream.

All dreams are wish fulfillments, Freud argued, and it was easy to see the wishes in this dream. First, the dream snake was very big, so I was telling myself I hadn't been silly to be afraid. I made the dream snake big enough to be a genuine threat. But, paradoxically, the dream was also granting my larger wish to be safe from this hoped-for real danger. This is why it was day in the dream and I was wearing about-the-house, or safe, clothes. Whenever I go out to the fields I change to my danger clothes—long jeans and long-sleeved shirt to protect me from thorns, poison ivy, crazed frogs, all those dangers out there. The clothes in my dream represented safety.

Freud's theory argues that the source of a dream is residue from the day before but that this residue is always used by the dreamer to recreate potent ideas hidden within the dreamer. According to the theory, I had merely used the snake of the day to dream about deeper, latent issues. It seemed to me Freud hadn't accounted for real snakes in real basements in his theory, but since he is one of the pivotal thinkers of the modern era, I decided to give him the benefit of the doubt and try to puzzle out what else the dream could mean. Animals can be symbols—of people sometimes. Could the snake in my dream have been someone?

If so, that someone would have to be male. No culture, primitive or modern, has failed to find a correlation between snakes and penises, although most mythologies have dwelled upon that organ's link to water, not babies, water presumably being the scarcer resource. Whenever snakes appear as god or symbol—in Egypt, Japan, India, Australia, pre-Columbian America, Europe, including Greece and Rome—they usually represent water or rain, at least initially. During the heights of Grecian and Roman civilizations, the snake declined from rain god to simply general benefactor. It became the custom in Roman families to feed a snake and encourage it to live in the house as a protector. In Roman art these household snakes were sometimes pictured with human faces and wings.

Even in these advanced societies, the reliability of the water supply was one of the things snakes were supposed to protect. I wondered if I had created a snake god in my dream, one that promised me rain. I had been hurt by the drought. I raised trees; half my orchard looked dead, and most of my black walnuts were under stress. Rain weighed on my mind. Was the dream a wish for relief from the drought?

Perhaps, but this seemed too simple. The rain symbolism wouldn't explain my waking horror at the sight of the snake. Nor would it explain why the dream temporarily relieved my fear. I recalled reading once that the modern vendetta against snakes is essentially Christian in origin. India, which has far more poisonous snakes than the West, has nothing quite like our snake hatred. In most of the world's mythologies, snakes can be both good and bad. Hermes and Medusa, for example, were both originally snakes reworked into human form by the Grecian anthropomorphic impulse, but retaining snake elements—Hermes with a snake-twined staff, Medusa with that hairdo. Hermes was benign, Medusa dreadful. They are only two of many good and bad snakes coexisting in the world's pantheons. Only in Christian tradition does the snake generically represent evil. Even the Hebrews, whose snake in the Garden is a peg in Christian thought, saw their snake as just a mischievous snake, not as Evil Incarnate.

Politics may have been the source of the Christian attitude toward snakes. In the debasement of Roman culture that preceded Rome's fall and coincided with the early history of the Church, there grew up a snake cult devoted to Dionysius which, well, was disgusting, even to Romans. The Church viewed all forms of animal worship as pagan or, to put it in political terms, as competition to be vanquished. So they took advantage of this particular fringe, which then (as it would now) offended the mainstream, to strengthen their attack on all competing, non-Christian ideologies. To bolster their position, they began to characterize the snake in the Garden as the devil. To wean people away from their attachments to the protector snakes of Roman family tradition, they simply converted these to guardian angels. The face and wings were retained in

Christian art, but the lower snake bodies became robes with elaborate folds, or cuddly babies.

By the Middle Ages a snake in Christian art always symbolized evil. The snake's connection to good had been diminished and its link to evil enlarged simply by deliberately altering the symbols. Who today seeing a Christmas crèche ever suspects that the angel above it was once a snake in the grass? Residues of this Christian iconography must lie behind much of the modern horror of snakes, a dread Freud described as "nearly universal." It certainly could explain why my own waking response was instant horror and why the fear seemed to arise outside of me. I was raised a Christian. I'd been told about the devil.

But what this idea couldn't explain was why my dream was peaceful. If my unconscious had sense enough to be terrified of the snake/devil when I was awake, surely that sense would prevail in sleep. Perhaps then my dream calm lay in yet another idea attached to snakes, one familiar to me also. Early man had been fascinated by the snake's ability to shed its skin and believed this made it immortal. He was jealous of this gift and was puzzled why the gods or God had given it to snakes and not to man.

The explanation in a variety of cultures, but especially in the Middle East, was that the snake had been sent as a messenger to give immortality to man but decided to keep it for itself. In one version of this story, a Promethean-style hero, after tremendous effort, obtains immortality from the gods. On his way to give it to man, the hero stops to bathe. (That link to water again.) While he's in the pool, a snake slips up and steals the immortality. So pervasive is this theme, especially in Semitic legends, that some scholars argue the Biblical version may be truncated. The original, preliterate version of the Hebrew story might have been: God sent the snake to tell man there were two trees in the Garden, one that led to death and one to life everlasting. The snake was supposed to tell Adam and Eve which tree to choose, but it decided to eat of the Tree of Life itself and deliberately sent Eve to the wrong tree. How different civilization might have been if this had been the dominant definition of man—as unlucky, not sinful.

At any rate, the snake's bid for immortality is a nearly universal myth and certainly one I was aware of when I created my dream snake flowing over and over in that sideways eight—a symbol of infinity. When I connected the dream snake with that, I recalled with a start the one person in my world who has access to infinity: my father, who died a dozen years ago, whose name was Harry, which sounds like Barry, and who often told me about a pet bull snake he had kept in the basement when he was a boy. He said it slept on a *ledge* down there above his mother's canned goods. The dream snake must have been my father.

If so, that explains why the snake would not come upstairs nor could I go down there. He is dead. He cannot come up from the grave, nor can I visit him. But in the dream, even though I was not permitted to see him, at least I had the comfort of knowing he had visited this farm. Time and time again my mother and I have told each other how much he would have loved this place. It's always made me sad that he died before I lived here. In my dream, at least, this wish was granted. It must have been important to me, judging by the depth of my calm when I awoke.

This venture into analysis worked very well to postpone my having to cope with reality, but did nothing to solve the problem. I stalled that entire morning. It was almost noon before I forced myself down into the basement. First I put on my danger clothes plus steel-tipped boots and rawhide gloves. I was hoping somehow Barry had managed to turn around and go back out the hole. But the ledge was so narrow; he could have fallen off.

Down the stairs. Open the door to the newly named Barry's room. Look on the ledge. No snake. Look behind the door. No snake. Peer up the cool concrete steps. No snake. Study the room, still hesitating in the doorway. Count the number of places he could have crawled into to hide. Six. Close the door. Go back upstairs.

I could not enter the room.

That afternoon I had just gotten to the part in the story where I say, "looked like corrugated cardboard," when the friend I was telling interrupted me: "A bull snake!" he said. "You are so lucky. You will never have a mouse or a rat or. . ."

I was miffed. Not only did he steal my punchline, but he delivered a sermon I'd already read. "I know," I said. "Now how do I get him out of my basement?"

"Oh, he got out the hole okay. Those snakes are constrictors, pure muscle. He can turn around and crawl over himself. He's not down there. How big was he?"

"Over five feet."

But the next friend's reaction was, "I've often seen snakes fall. He's probably still down there. How big is he?"

"Almost six feet."

"No, he can easily do a one-eighty. He's not down there," said my brother. "How big was he?"

"About six feet."

"Are you afraid of snakes?" was the next friend's reaction. His tone suggested he'd read the *Book of Lists* and knew what I knew, that fear of snakes is not a top contender for most popular phobia.

"Yes I am," I said defiantly.

Mercifully this friend then said, "I am too."

"Reminds me of the time I was fishing and saw seven cotton-mouths 'round me and. . ." More than one friend reacted to my snake this way—with snake stories that had real terror in them. Like waking up with a snake curled on your stomach. Or having one crawl over your hand. Or flinging one away only to have it pop straight up to fall right back down on you. And so on. Made my snake in the basement seem quite dull.

"You'll never come visit me anymore when I tell you what I found in my basement," I told my mother.

"Oh, God, not a rat," she said.

"No, a six-foot bull snake."

"You're so lucky. Did Dad ever tell you about that bull snake he. . ."

It took about two weeks to tell and retell my story and learn that opinion was divided as to whether there was a snake in my basement. During this time I tried to investigate and remove each of the six hiding places. I put my student odd-jobbers to work on the first spot, some shelves, warning them in advance that Barry might be down there and to be nice to him, he was a friend of mine. They came tearing excitedly up the stairs to tell me he wasn't there, one shouting at me, "I'm so disappointed. I really, really wanted to see him."

Another hiding spot was under the freezer I asked some workmen to move for me. Later I asked one if he'd seen a snake down there. "No."

And so it went until the last hiding site remained. I had cleaned up two sites myself by then. Each time I worked in my steel-tipped boots and rawhide gloves, body tense, ready to run screaming from the room if I saw him. Each time I moved a bit of debris and saw nothing, I heaved a sigh of relief.

As I readied myself to tackle this last site, I had an unexpected thought: What if he wasn't there? Odd thought. I was hoping he wasn't. Yes, but if he wasn't, then all my reactions of the past two weeks were pure foolishness. Empty emotion. An exaggeration of nothingness. Pointless. It was enough of a dilemma to give me an excuse not to clean up the site for another day.

I thought then of a painting I had seen a few months before in the Art Institute of Chicago. My mother had called and repeated the familiar "Are you ever going to come visit us?" For once I'd said yes and we started talking about what we would do. I said I mustn't go to the Art Institute this time because I always go there and really should try to do something else. She said in all the years she'd been working in the Loop, she'd never gone there.

So, of course, we went to the Institute. The last painting we saw, titled *The Grey Image*, was in a room by itself. I don't remember the name of the artist, but I will never forget the painting. Only eight people were allowed in the room at a time to see it, and a sign outside warned, "Please do not lean on *The Grey Image*." The room was darkened, except for the image, which had a striking luminosity. Its texture precisely matched my basement walls and held me with the same fascination.

But also drawing my attention was something else, an oddity. There was a perceptual distortion in the image and I began trying to figure it out. Was the image suspended away from the wall? I put my head against the wall trying to see behind it. No, the image was on the wall. Everyone else in the room was also trying to solve the puzzle. And then, sign or no sign, I touched the image, laughed, and called my mother over. "Watch this," I said. "See my hand go up and down. See my hand go out and in," and I put my arm through the painting. There was nothing there. It was a hole in the wall, and when I put my head in the hole I could see the lights that made the illusion.

At that, everyone in the room reacted, but to my surprise they were angry. They'd been fooled. Here they were, the trusting art gazers, willing to be awed before art, the sort who are serious about wines and books, who discuss films not movies, who pretend not to watch television, who don't like to be fooled by their art museums. "How typical of American art," said one in an I-wasn't-fooled-I'm-an-intellectual tone. I was bewildered. Why had the image ceased being real for them because it was done with lights instead of paint, as if the awe they wanted to feel would be something in a painting and not in themselves?

To me, it had been not only a pleasant image, but a fine joke. Yet take me out of art and put me in a real basement, and I had lost the perception. Fear of snakes, like awe of art, had been for weeks a nugget around which I had built a community of interest and renewed a link to the past, my own and others'. Far from being foolish, fear of nature, awe of it, was essential to this farm experience. Maybe that was the reason I stayed, for the way the fear linked me, not to nature, but to other people. Banshees and goblins in the night, like the image in the museum, have never been there.

But fear of them unites us and heightens life in ways common sense—reason—can never begin to fathom. I need not apologize for my fear; it had its use, and good thing, because Barry wasn't there.

That morning as I had dreamed and the puppy played, Barry had lifted himself and slid his forty-one spots one over another until his head reached the hole. He had squeezed through, dropping swiftly to the ground. As he'd moved through the short grass, perhaps the birds had stilled or else set up a racket of alarm. He would have passed a cedar on his way to the nearest bush, a lilac, slipped down a bank into tall grass and safety. I repaired the hole. Winter came. Somewhere in one of the dozens of dens that pocket my woods he slept. And I waited, certain now that I knew why I stayed on the farm. I hoped in spring he would resume protecting me. But I also hoped his cousins, the angels, would ask him if, this time, would he mind staying in the garage?

DEBRIS READER

CHAPTER ELEVEN

DEBRIS READER

I t was April again and as always on waking, I looked out my window. An ordinary enough routine, except for the view of garden, pond, woods, field and deer, pheasant, woodchucks, or occasionally a raccoon late to den for the day. On this morning, however, the view included Sam, my rooster, who should have been inside the chicken house protected from those raccoons. He was alone, pecking earnestly at something in the garden. I was sure I had shut him in the night before. I strained to check the chicken house and spent several seconds looking before I realized that the door was hard to see because the building was gone.

Completely gone. Nothing. A flat slab of concrete. The rooster. And me, screaming. In the night I had been awakened by a thunderous roar, something I'd never heard before but still knew had to be a tornado. I'd rolled from the bed and run downstairs but was too late to get to the basement. Instead I stood in a doorway, clutching the frame, as the house swayed and creaked. Through a window I saw a whitish mass. Storm sashes and gutters pulled off the house into the mass and hung suspended in midair until they and the mass disappeared. In seconds it was over. The house stood. I was quite clearly alive, although drenched in an acrid sweat. And, absurdly, I was sleepy. I stood stupidly in the doorway for a minute, then went back to bed. What else is there to do after a tornado?

So in the morning I'd not so much forgotten the storm, as never comprehended it. But I took it in now. The storm had lifted the chicken house—a huge building, wide as my own house; I used only half of it for chickens. It had come apart neatly at the corners and been dropped, a wall at a time, over several hillsides. Fiberglass insulation I'd stored in the other end was now draped over trees like Christmas tinsel. All my hens were gone. And I was screaming—hours after the event.

I could, even if screaming, see the tornado path clearly. When it passed by my window, it had shattered an apricot tree. Then it had passed the corner of the house, angling over the garden, pulling kitchen storm windows off as it went. It then uprooted a fence, shattered the corncrib, scattered a stack of firewood, and finally lifted the hen house. Lifted it. *Carried* it. Carried it across ten acres.

According to the Fujita-Pearson Tornado Intensity Scale, named, cleverly, for Pearson and Fujita, a tornado like mine that "damaged but did not destroy" well-constructed frame houses, snapped trees but did not uproot them, and demolished weak outbuildings like my hen house, would just be a piddling F-2 tornado: "Strong." My tornado would, the scale predicted, have had a wind speed of between 113 and 157 miles per hour, been less than fifty yards wide, and traveled on the ground at most a mile. Hardly worth screaming about.

The illusion of reason in the face of chaos has never failed to astonish or fascinate me. The perceptions of the Fujita scale were so radically different from those of the human screaming at her window. And yet both were equally irrational. The scale appeared rational enough when it lay innocently in my weather book. The chart heightened the illusion. The tables said the F-1, or "Weak Tornado," spins at exactly 73–112 mph. Not "about 70" or "a little more than 100." But 73–112. Yet tornado wind speed has never been directly measured. No instrument can survive the ferocious spin, nor is it common for a precision-minded scientist to be on hand to position an instrument package when a tornado, Weak, Strong, or Otherwise, strikes. Doppler radar in recent years has made some very good *estimates* of wind speeds possible, but actual measurement of a spinning tornado has eluded science.

Instead, the tornados are measured by giving people photos of damage caused by new tornadoes. They study the debris, matching the damage to previous storms. I had often thought I'd like to be a debris reader, having a formal duty to study chaos and give it a number. The Severe Tornado, F-3, 158–206 mph, would have torn the roof off my house. A Devastating Tornado, F-4, 207–260 mph, would have leveled the house. And an Incredible Tornado, F-5, 261–318 mph, would have lifted my house "clear off its foundation and carried it considerable distance." Not only that, my weather-watching handbooks explained, it would also have "badly damaged steel reinforced concrete buildings, tossed automobile-sized missiles a distance of 100 yards or more and debarked trees completely." And "incredible phenomena" might have occurred.

These phenomena are the stuff of folklore: Straws driven through trees. Animals picked up and found grazing, if muddy, miles away. Cows snatched from their stalls while the milker sits uninjured on a stool. Paint stripped off intact buildings. Houses completely demolished, but dinner left neatly at table, undisturbed and still warm. My tornado did leave a sack of chicken feed on the hen-house floor; the grain bin was gone, but the sack remained.

In 1899 reports of a Missouri tornado told of a woman who was carried about a quarter mile. She said afterward she was conscious the whole time and saw church steeples below her. She also saw a horse above her and prayed it wouldn't kick her. I would have been praying to outlive that horse. A 1966 Topeka, Kansas, tornado spread debris as much as sixty miles away from the impact site; a homemade chocolate cake, still on its plate, had been blown all the way to Missouri. My tornado did nothing so exotic. It didn't fly my chickens to Missouri. It just killed them.

By any standard my tornado was nothing special. It occurred in April. Most tornadoes occur in April, May, or June. It didn't kill anybody. Few tornadoes do. Lightning kills more people each year. It happened in Iowa. Iowa has more than sixty a year. My tornado was so boring it didn't even make the news. Even I knew it was a routine tornado.

But then I'd known a snake in the basement was no problem, either, yet managed to amuse myself for weeks as reason and instinct battled for the controlling insight about Barry. Reason appeared in control as I walked among the debris later, but it was, like the

Fujita-Pearson scale, an illusion in the face of chaos. I was stoic, studying the debris, assessing it, in a sense numbering it—until I came across the body of one of my hens. At that, I started to cry. Something unmeasurable had happened.

The geese had died of a virus the year before, so the chickens had been all I'd had left that seemed real to me anymore. With them gone the place was just a house with a big yard and I was F-3, F-2, F-1, F-nothing. Once again the question I'd calmed with Barry spun into troubling existence: What was I doing here? Perhaps I should have been grateful I and the house were not seriously harmed. Instead I stood by that hapless bird, surrounded by wreckage real and symbolic, and I cried. Why, why, why was this place so difficult? The weeds were winning. The power that dwells in fences and causes them to flop over was winning. The force that motivates water to penetrate basements was winning. The weather was winning.

In the depths of this hysteria another self within me began to act, or so it seemed because I "came to" later and was surprised at what "I" was doing. I was breaking kindling. This second self, an instinctive one perhaps, had noticed my brush pile was undisturbed by the storm. It used to be my routine to stop by this pile with every trip to the chicken house and break some brush into kindling. In the uproar and stress of recent years, I'd lost the habit and never regained it.

Now with my rational self roiling out of control, my instinctive self stooped, gathered some sticks, and began to break them. This other self automatically resumed my old technique of measuring three handspans, or a stovelength, before breaking each stick. This other self measured and broke, measured and broke, over and over many times. When I became aware of what I was doing, I was also deeply calm, alert, able to feel sun on my shirt and hear the orioles that had returned.

My mind was still not clear, but I did think at once this calm needed explanation. Most puzzling about the moment was its power. I was completely calm, rock calm, and knew it. I knew the calm would persist and reconnect with reason and lead to rational acts, like "call the insurance company" or "cut the apricot tree into firewood" or, above all, "stop the silliness of investing my self-concept in eleven dead hens." This all happened, but why? Obviously, I was acting partly from need for control. Even with mounds of timbers splintered around me, I knew and recognized the gesture as an attempt at order. In fact, especially with chaos around me, it was no particular wisdom to try to do something mundane. But why, this once, was routine so effective?

The "second" self? Did my instinctive self see kindling as a hedge against the winter, a symbol of survival? If so, there was an ancestral logic to my behavior. Existence itself once depended on routines this mundane. Religious care in performing acts tuned to the seasons led safely, if paradoxically, to an impermanent future – the winter. Observing the stars, planting at the right time, gathering and storing food and fuel – this worked, people survived. Winters would pass and the cycle begin again. There was no beginning or end. Routines progressed, became rituals and disciplines, but their progression was endless.

It had to be this cyclic quality I was reaching for when I instinctively broke my sticks, because my life had no link to literal winter. These are winterless times. We buy fresh food in January, adjust heat with dials, bundle ourselves just enough to survive the trek from house door to car door. My kindling was a game, a curiosity, a pretense. I had a furnace in the basement like everyone else.

Yet if there is no winter, still there are other routines, which, like primitive ones, are tuned to metaphorical seasons; that is, they progress, but the progression is endless. If performed with religious care, they lead safely, if paradoxically, to new beginnings. A friend who runs never stops at her prechosen level, but always pushes for new endurances. As soon as one goal is reached, suddenly she is talking about another. A dieter I know is truly serious – her eating habits have been realigned for life, and she is forever advising me to do likewise. A tennis player, a pianist, a carpenter, and a cellist

I know are just as serious; they practice daily. I have a friend who rises before breakfast to meditate; another who plays volleyball on Tuesdays; another who hikes in March, but prepares for this all year; another who reads a "good" book a week. None ever achieves enough to stop. Their private milestones arrive and pass, like winters, and their cycles, their disciplines, begin anew.

But they—we—often falter in our routines. I would not starve without my kindling, but still I had felt guilty not doing it. If my running friend skipped her morning jog or my dieter slipped into a junk-food lapse, then I heard about it. These were trivial lapses, yet these people experienced them so acutely they confessed them. The guilt never seemed to lie in the sight of the unread book, the mute cello, or my own shrinking kindling pile. It was deeper.

Is there some instinctual memory among us of when such lapses were paid for with life itself? Was I, when I broke my sticks, linked to those throngs of runners, comically unaware of each other bobbing in hundreds of parks? Together were we connected to our long-dead grandmothers who shared the routine of daily rekindling fires at dawn? Is the link, stretching from grandmother to grandmother, hearthfire to campfire, through time, a remnant of a past when the dangers were real and the disciplines exacting? Now manifest in a rainbow of sweatsuits, successful beyond describing—did any one link of this huffing chain ever suspect he or she might be trying to outrun the winter? Of course I was breaking kindling after the storm. I wanted to survive. Anyone with the will to live has some mundane routine—a hobby, an art, a cause, a home. If the will to survive is universal, might the rhythms of daily routine be its human expression?

But why the failures? The golf bag in the closet, the guitar on the shelf, the paints in a drawer, the dropped classes, the overslept mornings, the neglected brush piles. In our era, all urgency seems lost. Reason knows, if instinct does not, that winter is gone. Only in moments of crisis, when survival seems threatened, do we remember the past. I was breaking kindling to save my farm. Without the chickens, I'd lost reality. The loss was terrifying, the crisis real. I was trying to survive it, one stick at a time. In times of danger, perhaps the wisdom of the past overpowers the rational present and shows again the solution: rhythm, if serious, leading to safety. Breaking kindling was as rational as anything else I could have done.

But why the calm? Thanks to the chickens, the task had once been rhythmic. Thanks to the woodstove, the task was still impermanent. I'd had my paradoxical routines before the tornado. But instead of feeling deep calm, I'd been thoroughly bored. Boredom, not peace, is the usual outcome of routine, mine and everyone else's. Ignore the failures—the mornings when we didn't run or diet or complete the poem. Consider the successes, when we did brave the snow, skip the doughnut, or struggle with blank paper. The result, more often than not, was self-pity for the loss of one cinnamon danish with raisins. We admire ourselves for being disciplined when we torture ourselves with our routines, but the pride never really masks the fact that those rhythmic routines are real chores. Breaking kindling was boring.

Why was it different now?

My hands became tired eventually. I had to stop. I rubbed my sore knuckles and studied the pile. It was then I realized I had no idea how much work I had done. Normally when I broke kindling I would eye the pile as I started and eye it again when I stopped, mentally measuring my progress—giving chaos a number. I would note my accomplishment, reward my effort with an accounting. This time I'd forgotten to measure. In this oversight lay the calming power.

I'd experienced drudgery before because I measured. In this rational world, I have been taught the importance of measuring. Events unmeasurable whirl their consequences and we, the debris readers, assess them, F-2, F-3, F-forever, counting and believing we have a measure of control. My four-foot kitchen list of tasks I thought I needed to do was witness to my trust in that idea. We winterless children measure ourselves, plan, and take pride in results. We set, live by, and are sometimes consumed by goals, unaware that if routines derive from a primitive consciousness, then, like the storm spinning outside, they cannot be measured.

If routine is to have power, it might be an error to take those first jogging steps out the door and measure the distance. It might be wrong to diet and count the pounds lost. Goals measure nothing. A static number can have no meaning under the onslaught of sunrise and sunset and season upon season.

Artists I know had tried to tell me this. They routinely poured craft into their work even if few people could detect the subtleties of their skills. Still they reached for measureless perfection. The chain of grandmothers may have understood this too. At every estate auction I've attended, there were always hundreds of canned goods to be thrown away. These old women had processed and stored food because it was there to be harvested, and ignored the obvious fact that this exceeded their goal of simply feeding their families.

Serious athletes had tried to tell me the same thing, but their terms were confusing. I didn't understand. They said it "took a while," one had to "stick with" running or tennis or swimming a long time until eventually it became a way of life, a routine. They all stressed how long it took, how hard it was to reach this state of mind. Even dieters had tried to tell me the same thing, that nutrition was a state of mind, an attitude, which took a long time to master. Each of these enthusiasts had tried to convince me it was something within their discipline itself, intrinsic to art or running or nutrition, that led to this frame of mind.

But I suspected now that any routine had this potential, even volleyball on Tuesdays. Nor should it take as long as they say. It's just that, taught to value goals, we are blinded by them. Only if we persist long enough with a routine will instinct overpower reason and set goals in their place.

The time to reach this awareness might be shorter if we could grasp sooner that with routine, the real commitment is not to goals but to time, the ebb and flow of it, the rhythm, the power. How blind I'd been. I had never wanted a real farm or nature or its fear. I wanted time here, its rhythms, day in, day out, and if I didn't yet understand what that meant in practical terms, I could at the very least begin by tearing up my four-foot list.

It took many months to pick up the debris; my waist slimmed, my legs firmed, and I touted my "tornado spa" to friends. I did not replace my chickens, nor want to. My routines, as before the storm, were still rooted in the farm. They were less than before but that mattered less to me also. I was free of needing the place to be a real farm. That goal withered in the moment by the brush pile. But it had taken a tornado to move me to see.

FIRE AND ICE

CHAPTER TWELVE

FIRE AND ICE

S o time was my answer. Unfortunately, there was one small fragile assumption in my reasoning that collapsed quickly. These were not winterless times. I always hired someone to cut my firewood for me, but one year I hired a man who was good-natured, hard-working, and a total fool. Cut the logs in two-foot lengths, I told him, because my stove was twenty-six inches wide inside. Obviously the stove was meant for two-foot logs, plus two inches maneuvering room. But my wood-cutter decided, why waste those two inches? He cut every log exactly twenty-six inches long. He measured. I stood with slack-jawed incredulity as he proudly showed me the piece of metal he used for a cutting guide.

His misguided zeal meant no log fatter than six inches would fit in my stove. Wrestle or wedge or tug, I couldn't get a thick log in and still shut the stove door. My supply of thin wood dwindled until finally one night in January I had only thick wood to burn. Of course this was the same night the windchill reached an unprecedented minus 81 (or minus 26 degrees plus 30 mph wind speed). The radio bristled with alarms: "Don't go outside, exposed skin freezes in ten seconds. Bring your dogs and cats inside. Don't try to drive—the roads are drifting shut."

My pickup wouldn't have started at those temperatures anyway. The nearest house, a quarter mile away—shouting distance on a summer's day—was too far to walk in this blizzard. Rescue-squad snowmobiles couldn't get to me in this weather if the house got cold. Iowa winters can be bad—Iowans take a perverse pride in that—but this was one for the record books, and I was out of usable wood.

I hadn't used the furnace since the stove was installed. I'd rewired the thermostat myself when we tore out the wall. At the time it didn't occur to me to test it. Now I tested. The furnace came on — to my great relief. But the oil tank was almost empty. Did I have enough fuel to last the night? Even if I did, would power lines hold out all night? Outages are routine in Iowa blizzards. That was one reason I'd switched to wood.

Fuel and power did hold out that long, frightening, sleepless night, but not fear. By morning that fear had turned to rage. My woodcutter's well-meaning mistake could have killed me. I made up my mind that night to get a chain saw and learn to use it. Several weeks went by before I followed through because I was scared of the idea. I'd heard too many stories of trees dropping on buildings — or loggers; of saws kicking back and slicing off arms and legs and heads and such. After an expert siege of stalling by reading half a dozen books, I finally bought the saw, took it home, fueled it, adjusted the chain, and — heart pounding from fright — pulled the starter cord.

It didn't start.

Once again fear was replaced by rage, a roaring helpless anger much worse than that the night of the blizzard. After four days of pulling I took the machine back to the dealer. The compression was set incorrectly, he said, and after his slight mechanical adjustment, a feather-light pull of the cord would start it. I took the saw home and cut every one of my twenty-six-inch logs in half.

The logs lay in pleasant chaos against the snow, sawdust splayed in liberating patterns. I'd done it. Inside, I built a fire in the stove and, master of my universe, considered what I'd learned: That helplessness led to fear and rage. That knowledge controlled the rage. That, for me, it took a true crisis to push me to risk acquiring knowledge. I was going to change that. I would not wait for crises anymore. I would begin now. With the chain saw. I would fear no tree.

I started with small trees, obviously. When I began to feel confident, I was ready for the capstone hurdle in my chain-saw curriculum: a real tree, a thick one. Since the tornado had ruined the old apricot tree, I chose that for my first big tree. I fueled the saw and marked the felling notch with chalk. In theory, this notch, opposite the cutting side, controls the direction of the fall. When I lifted the saw to cut, I realized the tree was wider than my blade.

Of course there are techniques for cutting such trees. My chainsaw book had a whole chapter on them, but I didn't understand a word of it. For months that tree mocked me. Was I in control of this place or not? If I couldn't get rid of a tree, I'd never be free. Any leaky pipe, torn shingle, or clogged gutter could defeat me unless I mastered tools and skills. I asked my brother to visit me so he could take me to the hospital if the tree dropped on me. Didn't I think I should get a professional? I heard him start to ask, and then with that instinct siblings have sometimes, he didn't say it. He realized I had to cut that tree myself.

He and his wife stood solemnly nearby—but out of reach of the tree—while I tried to rehearse the cut in the air. Start by a plunge cut, the book instructed, which meant touch the trunk with the tip. In another chapter the same book stressed *in italics* that touching *anything* with the tip invited deadly kickback. After the plunge cut, I was supposed to work the saw at an angle until a hinge was formed. This was the part that baffled me. I gave up and decided just to begin. The plunge went well and as I cut I began to see what the book meant. I cut until I thought I'd formed a hinge. The technique is supposed to be, cut toward and slightly above the notch until just enough wood is left to pivot the tree in the right direction—away from the cutter and in line with the notch.

I stepped back expecting the tree to fall. The huge tree groaned and leaned toward the notch, widening my cut by a few degrees, but it didn't fall. My hinge was too thick. The wood, although under stress, could not break. I waited. The tree stabilized.

What was I to do? There was so much tension in the wood that if I came closer to cut and the tree snapped while I stood there, it might spring up and club me. On the other hand, if I didn't cut, I risked letting a gust of wind push the tree the wrong way against my house or me. I walked to the tree, knelt down, and looked into the cut. After a few moments' deliberation, I restarted the saw, reinserted it, and cut. In seconds it was over; the tree fell perfectly in line with the notch, its branches sighing as it sank. No kickback or springback—nothing. Except for the intermission, it was a textbook cut. I had done it.

We poured glasses of sherry all around to toast the tree and me, although my hand trembled so violently I could barely pour. My brother lifted an eyebrow at that. He couldn't know that I believed my life had never been so much in danger. Or so much in control. Chain-saw mastery gave me confidence to tackle the rest of it. Electricity. Carpentry. Plumbing. The internal combustion engine. I began with carpentry because I happened to have some tools and a piece of plywood in the basement. Again, it took days to get up the nerve, but finally I dusted off the circular saw that had lain unused in the basement for years. A carpenter friend had given us that saw. Mark used to run it occasionally, but I'd never even held it in my hands before.

I ran it without a blade first to see if it worked. It sounded fine. Once again I stalled by reading and rereading manuals. Eventually I drew a line on the plywood, put a blade in the saw, and cut. And laughed. I have known how to sew since I was ten, so I realized, as the saw bit into the wood, that I knew how to cut. Running that machine was identical to running a seam. The tension in my hands, the concentration, the angle of my head as I watched the cut—all were exactly like looking around a presser foot on a sewing machine, though it took slightly more hand strength. But not a lot. If I'd known carpentry was sewing, I'd have tried it sooner. I would learn this over and over. Everything resembled something else. I had only to see the similarities to control the skill. Electricity was plumbing without the water. Plumbing was sawing pipes instead of trees. I studied electrical books and replaced old ceiling fixtures. I studied plumbing books and redid pipes in the kitchen. I studied two-cycle engine manuals and...

And was baffled. So much for burgeoning control. The machine that halted my progress was an old six-horsepower weed mower that wouldn't start. It, like the saw in the basement, sat unused. A neighbor thought the carburetor might be gummed up because it had sat so long and why didn't I try cleaning it with Gumout. I bought a can of Gumout and read the instructions: "Remove air cleaner and clean outside of the linkage." (Linkage???) "Spray down the throat." (Throat???) "Spray both ends of the choke valve." (???) Meaningless jargon. I just sprayed everything in sight, waited until the machine was dry, and pulled the cord. The machine started.

The thrill I felt at its roar exceeded even the thrill of conquering the apricot tree. The next year I would disassemble that same baffling carburetor, clean it, reassemble it, and again start the engine. I knew how. Friends shrugged or smiled whenever I tried to tell them about the mower. From their point of view, no rational being should pursue happiness with a can of Gumout. But I was. I, with a few tools and a can of this or that, was learning to be free. After a time, I felt competent enough to look forward to winter, especially blizzards.

The wind howled, but I had wood for heat, kerosene for light, water, a pantry full of nonperishable food, and always books. I could last for weeks. Blizzards were times of cozy respite from daily life for me. The perfect excuse ("I'm sorry I couldn't get to your meeting—the blizzard, you know"). More than that, the times after the storms were purest beauty. Sunrises and sunsets were more colorful after a blizzard. The soft sculpting of the drifts pierced by the rhythmic stitchery of the cornstalks, the intensity of the night stars, the comic antics of the dog as she bounded into and out of snow mounds, the crunch of the frozen crusts, and, best of all, the eerie silence. The silence was absolute, as if the wind had exhausted every sound-making creature and force, including itself. And yet once, on a night of this utter stillness, I heard a faint hum. I think it was the earth spinning.

All the observations of climatologists I read those years pointed toward the return of an ice age. The sun was thought to oscillate or pulse periodically, and whenever a pulse coincided with shifts in the earth's geomagnetism, an ice age occurred. If these measurements and theories were correct, the warmer part of the current postglacial era was over and the grip of ice would slowly be returning over the next ten thousand years—if the greenhouse effect of civilization's carbon dioxide didn't melt it all first.

I could wait to see which force won. Cozy and free and in control inside my sanctuary, I felt I could deal with either greenhouse or glacier, fire or ice. They were one and the same, weren't they? Everything resembled something else. The times snowed-in were luxurious times of reflection. Mostly I thought about my own oscillating perceptions. With the felling of the apricot tree, I had seen how every idea I'd had about this place had changed over time. With the cutting of my first sheet of plywood, I'd seen how every shift in perception resembled the others. In my time here, winter had become beauty, Gumout happiness, goals time, snakes angels.

The windmill had begun in my mind as magic, become a symbol of impending loss, and now stood as testimony to my indecision about the future. Stone had become dream, ideal had become real, herbicides had become trust or lack of it, geese had become awareness of my own troubled marriage. The forester had changed from living myth to scientist in my mind; Mark had changed from lyrical idealist into a living myth. All shifts were the same shift, but all had shifted. Nothing I believed when I first saw the windmill was unchanged. Every perception had changed with time. And if the moment by the brush pile meant anything, perhaps it was "time" I needed to see all along.

But seeing was difficult in this place. My April tree-planting moment aside, clarity had not come easily to me. I began to use my blizzards to try to see time. I gathered armloads of books from the library and stacked them by my stoveside chair—the same one I had fled the night of Barry's visit—now my blizzard-watching chair. Even my chair had changed with time.

The Library of Congress had confidently assigned time a number, one a little more complicated than F-2 or F-3, but still a number—

BD638. The books I found housed there all began with a warning that time was mysterious, a problem for all ages, especially perplexing for our own. The occupants of BD638 argued that preliterate cultures thought time was all at once. Past, present, and future were the same and existed simultaneously. I thought I could grasp that. My windmill was past, present, and future to me. Its now-silent frame was equally a reminder of my choice to have a future here, and of my past here too.

Primitive cultures saw their all-at-once time quite literally. Dead ancestors did not cease to exist, primitives thought. They were changed, but not gone, and so had to be fed. The future, or fate, was no less concrete, and was often felt magically in the present. A hunter would say he felt his prey before the encounter. A woman would say she knew in her womb of her future son's future death in future battle.

Daily experience may have been distinct from this mythic sense of past and future, but through rituals and festivals, mythic time shaped daily time. Mythic time was real. I have a friend from Ghana who grew up in a tribal culture. During the festivals of her girlhood, she recalls, the women of the village would take food into the Ancestors' Hut. Some time later they would come out and the food would be all gone. "I would be so scared—I didn't want to grow up and have to go in that hut," she told me. She laughs whenever she tells me stories like this, as if she's proud to be free of something foolish. But I marvel that once the past and its ghosts were as real to her as our moment talking across a table now. Whatever "now" was.

The split between practical daily and ritualistic mythic time became more urgent to explain as civilization developed. I could grasp that too. In a sense, a difference between Mark and me was that I was practical and he was idealistic. In terms of time, I was now and he was then. Which one of us was out of sync with reality? In this era the now seems to have an overwhelming power over thought and perception. But what is "now," when even the briefest thought takes time to frame? Why is the past remembered, the present ex-perienced, but the future unknown? Why is time in one direction, always toward the future? What of change and its twin, the illusion of constant reality? If all things change—now I am an infant, a child, an adult—then what is the I that does not change? How can there be change and not change?

These three issues—the "now," the direction of time, and change—were burning questions for ancient cultures. Could time stop? And if it could, was there anything they could do to prevent this end of the world? Sacrifice sheep? Hum on a hilltop? Dance, dance, dance, as if life itself depended on it? In the news every year there are stories of harmonic convergences and such. The questions were still real, weren't they? The now was a good mystery to ponder in the time-stopping peace of a blizzard.

In Egypt the answer to these worries was to assume time could not end. Time was timeless. Egyptian life was dominated by the Nile, which, like the sun, was born and died and born anew end-lessly. The sun relived every day. Live and die, live and die, over and over without end. This was time. Osiris, which means fresh water, was the creator. And Re, which means sun, was the first divine pharaoh. Beyond these firsts was no ending. Egypt was rare among cultures because it did not fear the end of the world. Per-haps they had such confidence because their culture was stable and secure, thriving for over twenty-five hundred years before the final Greek conquests. In such a context, the debris and up-heavals of daily events were momentary flashes in a timeless universe, variations on a theme.

China, like Egypt, was blessed with a stable and isolated culture. It, too, rooted its ideas of time in the cycles of nature. But the topography was more complex than Egypt's. The Chinese lived with craggy mountains, hills, woods, river valleys, and extremes of temperature. They saw infinite diversity in nature where Egypt had seen a monochromatic sameness. So time to the Chinese was a complex of patterns.

The Chinese alone of the early cultures had no creation myth. Nor a creator. What existed was constant rhythmic change, season upon season, day upon day, all part of an organic whole. The real world was not "momentary flashes," but pattern. All events were part of some rhythm, even if a careless observer could not detect the harmony. One of these patterns, the Chinese decided, was duality—male/female, night/day, good/evil, (meaning/lyric?). A key duality, of course, was beginning/end or as their *I Ching*, Book of Changes, put it, "beginning anew at every ending." If the world did end, another would begin.

Time as rhythm was an idea that mandated curiosity. If all events, no matter how chaotic or inconvenient, were part of a rhythm, then the next step was to be curious about the rhythm. "What is the harmony?" is almost the same question as "Why did it happen?" or "How did it happen?" The Chinese search for harmony stimulated careful observation. They developed science. They also were one of only two ancient cultures to develop history as an inquiring instead of dogmatic discipline. Their history was meant to be researched, not believed. It was not blasphemy to doubt the old testaments.

The Greeks were the other culture that was curious instead of dogmatic about the past. Their word for "inquiry" or "research" was *historie*. But the Greeks chose to brood about the irreversibility of events instead of the cycles of nature. They had gods and a creation myth, but their gods experienced day-to-day events. Their gods had lives. Things happened. The gods were immortal, but not changeless. Things did not unhappen or happen again, to gods or mortals. Events occurred. Time progressed. History was a line of individual moments of the past stopping at the present.

To the Greeks moments might seem to be similar. Spring or dawn may return, but it is always a new spring, a new dawn, unique, never to be repeated. In other words, the Greeks believed in experience. Time, then, was what a person made of it. The future might be shaped, changed. A person collected a lifetime of experiences, which could be carried into the future only through teaching. The future, thus, depended on the past. Again, it was a point of view that permitted inquiry. The future was changeable if the past and present were understood. Thus the Greeks, like the Chinese, developed science. They needed the information to control their fates.

Indian thought saw time not as rhythm or line, but as the fundamental corruptor of insight. Time blinded perception. Time was to be transcended. Events of life were chaos and noise, not existence itself. Time was like a river; the roaring waters pass and flow, but the river remains. On the surface this seems another version of Egypt's timelessness, but with this distinction: All change was part of the unchanging, like patterns on a fabric. If we are distracted by the patterns, we do not see the fabric. The problem is perception. Only by transcending the illusion of change does the Indian perceive changelessness. All events and thus all lives are linked to the fabric of the cosmos, the Absolute. But individual lives, like threads in a garment, were just a sampling of lives existing repeatedly in time. One was to be reborn and reborn and reborn until one sees the unchanging. To be fascinated by events is to be blind. And mortal.

These four ideas of time—Timeless, Rhythmic, Linear, or Unchanging—in one form or another define time in modern cultures, although there is one minor variant of the Greek version that also has had some modern impact. The Hebrews, like the Greeks, saw time as linear, but their history resulted from a covenant. There was a beginning. There would be an end. This was promised. A culture's idea of time to a certain extent defines what its people can know or become. The Greeks, Chinese, and Hebrews were careful to record history as accurately as possible, to locate events in time because to them this was the path to insight and mastery of nature. But the Egyptians and Indians wrote histories that were fanciful—works of art, not inquiry—because fascination with observed reality would blind them to the truths of nature. The differences profoundly shaped each culture's ideas of reality. It's fascinating when different ideas collide in the modern world. The so-called channellers who try to communicate with their past lives in this country—how Grecian/linear that is, to assume their past lives are unique and so worth the curiosity. In Indian thought, such effort is to miss the point, to see threads when one should be searching for fabric.

As for me, my blithely deciding to abandon goals in favor of time, was, I saw from these four ideas, actually a decision to re-examine reality itself. Was my tornado a momentary flash? It didn't make the news; so this made it Egyptian. Was it part of some har-mony? I had linked it to patterns in my life and so made it Chinese. Was my tornado unique? I had recorded every detail, the windows torn off, the trees snapped, the chickens killed. That made it Greek. Was it a message? That made it Hebrew. Was it part of my unchang-ing commitment to this farm? My searching in it for something to justify my choices to others? Perhaps that made it Indian. The changelessness of change. I stayed on and on.

But if my tornado was all these things, what then was time? Or reality? For most of time, whether timeless or rhythmic, linear or unchanging, there wasn't much in the so-called real world to challenge any of these ideas. Belief could flourish with little in the way of facts to challenge it. Until recently. That child of Greek and Chinese curiosity, science, has redescribed time. And reality.

The first idea to waver under the pressure of science was that of "a long time." There had been suspicions that the earth was old since the Islamic ascendancy of the tenth century. The Muslim Avicenna, writing just before A.D. 1000, observed that water eroded hills, sometimes slowly, sometimes rapidly, depending on soils. He thought some mountains were formed this way but that, "It would take a long period of time for all such changes to be accomplished."

These suspicions did not become science until the century of geology. In 1830 Charles Lyell published his *Principles of Geology*, which argued that—given enough time—the shape of natural forms could be explained by natural processes. Enough time, however, was millions of years. Charles Darwin was an assistant to Lyell.

It would be his observation that species change and adapt too. Given enough time.

The shock of millions of years was trifling compared to what this, the century of physics, revealed. In the 1920s Edwin Hubble confirmed that there were millions of galaxies in the cosmos. Furthermore, when he measured the Doppler shift from their light, he discovered that they were moving away from us at great speed, like debris from a bomb explosion, a Big Bang. In the 1960s, background radiation, the residue from this explosion, was discovered, confirming to most scientists' satisfaction that the bang had indeed happened. Billions, not millions, of years ago.

Even if there was a lot more time to time than imagined before, still it was assumed to be absolute. A minute was a minute, a day a day, and a light year a light year, anywhere in the universe—past, present, or to come. Einstein, though, argued that the rate time passed (as measured by a very good clock) depended on velocity and gravity. The faster one (and one's clock) went or the stronger one's gravitational field, the slower the clock (and time). Time was relative, but the differences in time were real. Thus if Barry went zipping about the universe at the speed of light and then returned to my basement, he would not have aged as much as I did. I would have experienced more time while he was gone. Time was relative.

The relativity of time was fairly easy to measure. The effect of velocity was measured by taking an atomic clock around the world by jet and comparing it with a similar clock that stayed put. The difference was in fractions of an instant, but there was a difference. The effect of gravity on time was measured by placing clocks at the top and bottom of a tall building. At the bottom, where gravity was strongest, time was slower—a microfraction of a second, yes, but still slower. Time was relative.

If time was my answer, I could not have picked a more slippery anchor. It made Mark's trenches in the garden look rational, especially if current notions of particle physics were added to the mix. Until the 1970s, cosmology, the study of the very largest thing in nature—

space—and particle physics, the study of the very smallest, rarely overlapped. But as particle physicists got closer to explaining the forces of energy and matter, cosmologists realized these forces could also explain the Big Bang, the beginning of Time. The four basic forces physicists had isolated were the electromagnetic force (which makes light shine), the strong (which holds atomic nuclei together), the weak (which causes particles to decay), and gravity (which causes matter to fall toward other matter). By the end of the 1970s, physicists were convinced that the first three, called elementary particle forces, were essentially the same force. (Time the unchanging?)

All three depended on interactions (called "events") of particles (which were not particles at all, but sometimes blips of pure energy called "quanta"). And there was a blizzard of interacting quanta. There was the photon, a massless, chargeless unit of light; and protons and hadrons and baryons and mesons made up of quarks, which could be either charmed or strange, up or down, or red, blue, or green—these colors not being "real" but concepts about quarks. There were electrons and leptons, muons and pions, neutrinos and bosons and vector bosons and virtual particles. Virtuals were particles that existed only a fraction of a fraction of an instant; they virtually didn't exist, but existed just long enough to enable an "event." And particle accelerators around the world found all these things, the tracings of their events etched on photographic plates. As the particles of the universe appeared, it became clear, at least to physicists, that the forces that formed them were probably, for one brief moment, at the time of the Big Bang, just one force, a Unified Field.

What was before the Bang is beyond the language of physics, but this Nothing must have been very unstable. Into this instability came Something, something as small as a virtual particle, smaller than the smallest atom, the smallest blip—massless, chargeless, whatever it was, it came. And *Boom*. But everything that is, is part of that Something. Perhaps.

The perhaps is because, one, protons do not seem to decay. And two—how did gravity fit into this? If all forces are one force there should be a "quanta" of gravity, a graviton, as yet undetected. And if all force were one force, all should decay, even protons.

Theory gauges the life of a proton at about 10^{27} years, which is several trillion times the age of the present universe. A billion trillion trillion, give or take a year or two. One way to test the theory is to wait trillions of years and see. The other is to put trillions of atoms together and see if one decays. In India (changeless time), Japan (rhythmic time), and this country (linear time) are buried in deep mines huge tanks of water lined with sensitive light detectors. If a proton decays, the new particles it emits should leave a wake of light. There have been a few such wakes detected, "candidate events," the physicists call them, but they want to be sure. So no such decay has been announced. If protons decay, then time will end much like the Hebrews say it began, in light.

But there may be another fated ending arriving sooner than dissolution into light. Gravity. Is there enough matter in the universe so that, when the inertia from the Big Bang finally plays out, the expansion of the universe would reverse? If so, then everything would begin falling toward everything else until meeting in a colossal Big Crunch. If the expansion does reverse, could time reverse with it? Could I meet myself in my chair some night?

It's theoretically possible. In a shrinking Universe, entropy might eventually have to reverse too. Entropy is the proportion of usable energy available in a physical system. It tends to rise over time, and like time, entropy is one way. But in a shrinking universe, given the conservation of energy, there must come a point when something has to give, entropy or the Universe. If one tries to put a quart of water in a pint jar, either the water must overflow, the jar must get bigger, or the water must shrink. Physicists think it most likely that the water—entropy—would shrink. Suppose, then, there was a planet of people living after the contraction began—would they then experience our past as their future? Like Merlin, would they live backwards? Of course they would feel the future as the future, just as we feel the past as the past, but which would it be?

These are not fanciful questions. Well, yes they are, but they are not unasked questions. These questions were raised at a conference at Oxford, England, in 1985. Physicists argued that even if time could reverse (and to help with the math they invented the tachyon, an imaginary faster-than-light particle with an imaginary mass, which by being faster than light would be going backwards in time, all the time), and if there could be people living in backwards time, it probably would never be possible to contact them and ask about their past (our future) because our world lines or locations in space-time could not cross with theirs. In theory.

At this point physics seems to me to have so left the realm of common-sense daily time that it makes the ideas of mythic time seem conservative. And yet I love to think about it. What if any of it is true? What if it's already happened? What if beyond our capacity to perceive, people are tumbling back over themselves? Maybe the Indian view is right: perception is the problem. What if we could perceive the world lines, the space-time of another universe? Perhaps all those UFOs and moments of clairvoyance and seeing of Uncle Wally's ghost—all those unexplained things that so fascinate tabloid readers—are just stray tachyons in the living room.

These are dangerous ideas, I know. There are just enough people who, hungry for answers, would believe this and organize channelling sessions to get in touch with these reverse-living peoples. Channellers are busy now trying to reach their past lives; if disappointed there (I was just a street sweeper?) they may try to reach their future lives, too, and maybe start a religion—or an investment firm.

I don't want that. I just want the question. What is time? And where is it going? Will it be unending, Egypt's timelessness? Will it be Crunch, a final Grecian linear ending? After the Crunch, will there be another Bang and the universe ceaselessly oscillating between Bang and Crunch, over and over in perfect rhythmic duality, a Chinese forever, every ending a beginning? Or will it be changeless, past and present one and the same, backwards and forwards, an Indian Absolute?

Only a primitive mind truly believes it can affect these forces of time, to dance on a hilltop and bring back the sun. But after my moment by the kindling pile, I can't dismiss the primitive mind. In our time, the primitive hunger for power over time is still strong. In Fairfield, Iowa, just fifty miles from my home is the Maharishi University. I visited them on a magazine assignment once. They were busily trying to assemble a permanent community of seventy-five hundred experienced transcendental meditators because their science had revealed that if the square root of 1 percent of the world's population meditated together, they could calm world tensions. I was skeptical of that science. It seemed to me to focus too much on evidence that supported their views. A true scientist looks for disconfirming evidence. But I had to admit, as they tried to save the world from ending, that they'd created something for themselves. I'd never met a group of people more happy, more at peace with themselves. They glowed with joy. And I, who could wonder about existence just because it was snowing, had no business judging anyone else's musings.

I did realize, as blizzards came and went (and so did the books), that none of these ideas, or any idea that seems to be final, is for me. And at last I know why. I love questions, not answers. Living myths, whether it's gardens they dig or hilltops they meditate on, have answers. Mainstream or fringe, answers are the end of questioning. No matter the topic—how to raise chickens or how the universe will end—once the answer is found, questions end. And when questions end, so does wonder. The living myths I have known, Mark included, needed some kind of answer, something to believe in. And I needed, just as strongly, the opposite. No wonder I caused pain. I cannot imagine a life without questions. Living is wonder. Time was not my answer, but my question.

I lived here, loved it here, because the questions were rich here. The herbicide/ethics question had taken days to resolve. The chickens/guilt and geese/water questions had reworked the universe for me. The snake/fear and windmill/commitment questions had fascinated me for weeks. The tornado/goals and now the blizzard/time questions promised to last a long, long time indeed. I exhausted the local resources of BD638 and began those of BF438, "perceptions of time," and still, happily, had questions. In fact, I have as yet reached only two conclusions. Neither could be ranked very high on a Fujita-Pearson Insight Intensity scale. At best they are F-2, Strong Notions, a long way from F-5, Incredible Solutions, but they will have to do. The first is, I've noticed that for all our indifference to it, winter returns and returns and returns. And the second is, I think someone should tell those people living backwards, whose future is our past, that they need to break a lot of kindling. The Wisconsin Ice Age is fast approaching.

CORN

CHAPTER THIRTEEN

CORN

Spring was returning slowly, as usual, as if it were reluctant to disrupt my sanctuary. I suppose I knew that my safe haven, immune from fire and ice, was not immune to anything. But as long as the snow was thick on the ground, I could pretend there was no world out there. The melting snow seemed an ally, dirty by day, but by night it turned to purest white dense fog, a final attempt at enveloping whiteness before growth and weeds and reality intruded. Normally I didn't mind the end of rest and reflection in March; the return of the first striped spring beauties in the woods compensated for the loss of peace. Most years I was tired of thinking by spring anyway. But this year was different. My contract was due in June.

Contracts are essentially mortgages paid directly to a private person rather than to a bank or lending institution. I'd been paying the widow all these years for the privilege of owning her home. It pleased me that the several thousand dollars interest I paid each year went to her and her children, instead of a bank. It seemed less like piracy. But our contract was maturing in June and under its terms I had to pay the balance in full, with either cash or a new contract or a conventional mortgage. I had no cash. The widow couldn't renew our contract because she had another, older contract coming due at the same time. A loan was my only option. So in March, as the mud billowed and flowed in yard and roadway, I invited a banker to inspect my home.

The banker arrived, wearing a three-piece suit. I had on jeans and a workshirt. He was wearing wing-tip shoes. I had put on rubber chore boots, in part because of the mud but also because I was boarding horses then and assumed he'd want to inspect the pastures. Until I saw those shoes. I said hello. He said the house was too far from town. I took a deep breath. This was going to be difficult.

I had asked my brother, the one with the MBA, what would happen if I didn't get a loan. I'd have to sell the place, he said, or declare bankruptcy. Sell my home? Leave this place?

"It's not too far," I protested. "It's only a thirty-five-minute drive from campus. That's nothing compared with the forty-five minutes it used to take to get across Manhattan when I lived in New York." I tried to tell him that having no traffic or stoplights was not a bad morning commute.

"Too far," the banker repeated.

As I opened the kitchen door for him, he let out a screech. "A red refrigerator?" He was plainly distressed at this breach of taste.

"Why not red?" I said. "The floor is gray, the appliances and walls white. The kitchen needed color."

"It's too small," he countered.

"I'm single. It's big enough for me."

He paused at the threshold of the dining room. "Have you considered carpets?" he said. At that I was angry. I thought it just plain ignorant not to know what a treasure I had in those hardwood floors. But the banker sniffed. Most people had carpet nowadays, he said.

Upstairs he asked why I'd taken my curtains down. There was neither house nor road out those windows. I didn't need the privacy. Why block my spectacular view with curtains? He thought I should get curtains.

The entire inspection went like this, the banker seeing one thing and I seeing another. I saw a charming old windmill. He saw a rusty piece of junk. I saw a field of wildflowers. He saw unmowed weeds. I saw a source of firewood. He saw a tangled copse of thorny brush. I saw quantities of free fertilizer from the horses. He saw filth. I saw a handy source of lumber for carpentry projects. He saw a collapsing shed. I saw a rare species of vireo safely nesting. He looked at me in horror to think that any civilized, educated human being would let filthy birds nest on her porch.

"If they were cowbirds or sparrows, I would have rousted them,"

I said, "but not vireos. They have such a pleasant song." But he wasn't listening.

I was not surprised to get a letter a few days later denying me the loan. Reason: insufficient collateral. The letter urged me to fix up the place and perhaps try again later. By "fix up" I assumed he meant mow my precious flowers, tear down my windmill, and get rid of my red refrigerator. I called my brother.

"He's not an ogre, Pat. They have to base their loans on actual value of the property, and part of the value is how well it meshes with current tastes. If most people like carpet, then bankers have to pay attention. That affects resale value."

"But I live here. They don't have to worry about selling it."

"They can't make loans on what you plan to do. They have to base it on the actual worth of the house."

He was saying that if I wanted to keep the place, I'd have to conform to the banker's tastes. At first I felt something like the general who said he had to destroy a Vietnamese village to save it. I was in a quiet rage as I mowed my wildflowers.

I couldn't tear down the windmill, but at least I ripped the vines off it. I burnt the shed, made the horses' owner find another place to board them, and hung curtains upstairs. I kept the red refrigerator, but hid it in the pantry. And when the vireos finished nesting, I invited another banker to appraise the place.

This one was less voluble. Whatever his thoughts, he kept them to himself. He measured the rooms slowly while I jabbered about the loveliness of the views, the sturdiness of the framing, and how much this place, my home, meant to me. His appraisal report a few days later described the house as "obsolete," mainly because the bathroom was downstairs and the bedrooms were upstairs.

After the third loan denial I began to face the reality—this was more than a clash of tastes. I was caught up in the farm crisis. Somewhere, something had changed. A list, abstract beyond imagining, had dropped, and my land, though unchanged itself, fell in value. The numbers were published every month in the paper—

land values had declined by such and such in such and such counties. No matter how much the place was worth to me, those impersonal numbers could cost me my home. For the first time I understood the bizarre scenes I'd been watching on television news. The wife would be weeping, the husband standing stoically by, as the sheriff ordered them off their land, cameras whirring. "We never missed a payment," the wife would wail, and I'd wondered then, how could they lose their land? Now I knew. My contract was due, but my land was worth less than what I owed. No lender could risk me.

Iowa farmers took to putting up crosses on courthouse lawns whenever any of them lost a farm. The suicide rate soared. I remember my neighbor's shock when she heard I was in trouble too. "Everyone's in trouble, everyone's in trouble," she kept repeating. I heard in her tone the thought that I was supposed to be immune. I wasn't a real farmer. I had a town job. I listened to her sympathy and pondered the irony that by losing my farm I would finally become a real farmer.

The tension in the country that year was palpable. If I ran my mind along the roads I traveled I could count alcoholism, wife beating, and suicide within families I knew personally. No doubt there was more of this among people I didn't know. Less than six miles away from me—in the neighborhood, in country terms— one farmer became stressed beyond sanity and killed his neighbor, his wife, and his banker before killing himself. One of my students covered the slayings for the student newspaper. In class that week she announced that her term paper would be late. Three murders and a suicide had been too much for her.

A few hours later she came by my office. "I want to apologize for my remark this morning."

I said no apology was necessary; under the circumstances, I understood.

"Then I don't want to apologize," she said. "I want to tell someone about my week." I gestured for her to sit down. She had been the first reporter on the scene, dashing out the moment the murder codes came over the police radio. As she got out of her car, she saw something on one of the bank's windows and thought it might be blood. At the window she stretched and leaned to look between the slats of the blinds and saw not only that it was blood, but that the body of the banker still lay slumped at his desk. She had gotten there so quickly he hadn't been moved yet.

"I can't describe my revulsion. I felt awful. I wanted to run or throw up. About a half hour later I came around the building again and lots of reporters were there, at the same window, leaning like I had been leaning, trying to see what I had seen, and I didn't know then which was more horrible, what I had seen, or them trying to see it. I don't think I want to be a reporter anymore."

She fell silent, waiting for me to say something. This is a hazard of the teaching profession, that even when there's nothing to say, one still is expected to say something. I said every journalist faced this sooner or later. There is something horrible about looking at people's pain for a living. You get through these bad scenes by believing it helps prevent future horrors. Perhaps her looking at that poor banker's death might save someone else's life, I told her.

In fact, I think that's what happened. The massacre was national news for several days and generated a number of specials on the farm crisis. Dan Rather came to the Midwest himself. So did Phil Donahue. Thanks to the public glare, proud, stiff-backed farmers began attending stress-management clinics and using suicide hot lines. The suicide rate dropped noticeably.

I am certain the courage of my student and others to look squarely at the horror helped. I told her I hoped she could keep looking. To be able to look at horror and feel horror was the only way to stop it. This might be her choice because of something else she told me. The banker had been one of those truly loved individuals, tireless in the community, active on behalf of farmers, a leader. The grief at his death was intense. Over a thousand people came to his funeral. During the service my student looked over at a *Des Moines Register* reporter she'd become friends with and saw that the woman—a professional—was crying. Somehow that made her feel better.

Yet what I did not tell my student, in advising her to look, is how difficult looking is. If my farm had taught me anything it was that perception is difficult. And rare. Only once had I seen my woods in their April beginnings. For all my study of it, I can't say I've seen time. Had I heard the earth spin? I certainly had never heard the corn grow. I glibly advise a life of perception without telling her that perception is the hardest of all lives. Why can't I hear the corn grow?

Farmers had told me for years that the young corn grows so rapidly it makes a sound, but I had never heard it. I had never seen the winter begin either. I think it starts in late August when the barn swallows organize on power lines. Every day their numbers increase on the lines, facing every which way. Every day it would seem to me that more and more of them face the same way on the lines, as if they were struggling to form a collective thought. But I never saw the moment when the thought was complete and the swallows flew. They would be there. Then they would be gone. Why couldn't I see that moment? Why is perception so difficult?

When it happened, though, perception changed reality. The fields were truly different after I learned some weeds could be eaten. The winter was truly different after I no longer feared the chain saw. My sense of control was truly stronger after I began seeing resemblances, carpentry to sewing, for instance. Differences in perceptions shaped reality too. Because of our conflicting perceptions, Mark was really gone. Because of conflicting perceptions, I was really losing the farm.

Physics in recent years has concluded that perceptions do affect reality. The act of observing a phenomenon changes the phenomenon, at least at the subatomic level. If perception changes reality, then obviously reality is perception. I had spent hundreds of hours seeking to control my world by mastering skills and knowledge, but what I needed to master was perception. The winds still howled when I knew how to cut wood, but my experience of those storms was now a time of beauty, not terror. The winter changed because perception changed. Or was it I that changed? What was real in this? Would I really lose the farm?

Through all of this I continued to drive back and forth to work each day, a distance too far in the bank's view perhaps, but comfortable for me. I think while I drive. When it became clear all was over, I put my house up for sale, although no buyers came to look. No one was looking at anything in this depressed area. I circulated my résumé, too, because I didn't want to stay in Iowa without the farm.

As I drove home one afternoon, I was lost in the usual chaos of mind that is the luxury of being trapped in a car: Did I need new tires, should I stop at K-Mart in the morning, was it time for a dentist appointment, was it too soon to mow the lawn, did my life mean anything, should I tell the director I'm looking for a job? Suddenly a hawk flew in front of me, almost striking the windshield. It was carrying a small snake in its talons.

Until the hawk startled me, I had been blind to the landscape. Now I noticed it again. The cornstalks were arrayed in stubby patterns because it was still too early to plow them under. Between the small woodlands, each with a stream, I saw once again the fields, all slightly hilly so the rows of stubble intersected and overlapped arhythmically, folding and crumpling toward an occasional horizon. The afternoon shadows deepened the colors, still neutral from winter. Evening mists were beginning to collect in the hollows. It was rare to see anything as dramatic as a hawk, although the week before I had seen five deer caucusing in a field. Hawk or no hawk, the landscape was remarkable enough—if I could look at it.

There are people I know who dread driving in the Midwest because mile after mile of corn is not scenery but agony for them. I don't see monotony in the corn. When I remember to look, I see an intricate and amazing wonder. Corn is an evolutionary masterpiece, engineered by people, able to live in semi-arid desert or tropical climates. It grows from Canada to Argentina, Maine to California, sea level to thirteen thousand feet.

Its seeds can remain viable for hundreds of years; it remains edible in storage for thousands. Corn fifty-six hundred years old was discovered in Peruvian archaeological digs and nearly lost again because expedition mules started eating it. One-thousand-year-old corn found in Arizona still popped when heated. Scientists don't know how the American Indians developed this wonder. No plant grows wild today that could be corn's precursor, although a perennial grass called *teosinte* may be a distant, very distant, relative.

These Indians created a plant totally dependent on humans for reproduction. The tough husks have to be removed and the hundreds of seeds dispersed away from the ear for the seedlings to germinate or survive. A field of corn is a human accomplishment, centuries in the making, an achievement more grandiose than the longest bridge or tallest skyscraper. It is the horizon itself that has yielded to human engineering, and I am impressed—when I remember to look. Why is perception so difficult?

In a few weeks the farmers would begin plowing and the stubble give way to a blackness so intense I thought the soil was asphalt when I first saw it. The blackness will look like velvet corduroy until smoothed by planters. A few days later a minute flush of green formed by billions of specks will stretch from horizon to horizon. The color will rapidly mass and thicken. For a day or two each stalk will stand framed by the soil, the blackness highlighting the curlicue of each tiny leaf. Then the color will overwhelm the soil, and the land will become a pure, intense green.

In the morning or afternoon light, the green will be tinged with gold and an odd maroon, a secret of the corn, visible only under strange light, and invisible to anyone who considers the corn dull. I am aware that this maroon green I pass each day erodes soil and produces more grain than the economy can absorb. But I cannot see it and not be awed by the skill and technical mastery that creates it. For better or worse, the farmers, moving back and forth in their fields, as I move back and forth on the highway, control the landscape. Like me, they work to control their environment. I with my saws, they with their massive combines and tractors, want to conquer the winter.

Like mine, their efforts may be meaningless in a world where value lies in distant numbers, not in effort or skill or commitment. Like me, they are vulnerable to forces they cannot control. Was that my mistake? Was the effort to shape my world pointless? Was the control I felt as I mastered my skills an illusion? I did not change the winter. I did, however, change my experience of it. It became a time of beauty, not terror. That was real, however. The happiness I felt was real. What went wrong?

I so enjoyed my illusion. I loved fixing up the place, though—it startled me to realize this now, with the farm slipping away from me—I did not reach that happiness until I pursued my skills without crises. I saw the resemblances, the patterns, felt the control only when there was no urgency, no project in mind. Is it the same with perception? Was my mistake that I am too dependent on the sudden hawk?

The things that most changed my perceptions were disruptions or even horrors—a snake in the basement, a tornado, a failed well, a divorce. No wonder seeing was difficult. Crises are rare. Cornstalks outnumber the mountains. The mundane outnumbers the peaks of experience. What if I learned to look when there were no hawks? Would the perceptions of others that can disrupt my life now lose power?

There is a moment in summer, in July, lasting only a day or two, when the corn tassels have fully emerged, when they are a perfect rich gold but the green of the corn has not yet begun to fade. Almost immediately after tasseling, the corn begins to turn brown, but for a day or two the green and gold coexist in the fields. This juxtaposition of color is explosive with intensity for me. Corn—ordinary, controlled, monotonous, economic corn—is for a moment thrillingly, purely incredible. I wait for the moment all year, and there have been Julys when I missed it, too intent on decisions about tires or K-Marts to look. What would happen if I learned not to wait for peaks, but to observe the ordinary? If I spend my life looking for peaks, even the peaks are hard to see. But if I look only for the ordinary, would it happen that I see? If perception is reality, then perception of the mundane may be freedom from chaos. Perhaps I would see the barn swallows leave.

In the end, literally days before I would have to default, buyers appeared. They thought the red refrigerator was cute. They loved the windmill and even talked of moving it over the well. Before they showed up I had lain awake for many nights wondering what would happen after the default. Would I lose my furniture? My pickup? My dog? Now I would keep not only all that, but my dignity too, plus have the comfort of knowing there were some people who looked at land as I did.

A few nights before I was about to leave, I stepped outside to escape the chaos of packing boxes inside. It was mid-May. The corn had just emerged. The night was still, almost a winter stillness. It was too early for frogs or crickets or whippoorwills. The wind chimes had been packed, although there was no breeze to stir them. But there was a sound, a rustling, like the crumpling of cellophane, and it was coming from the cornfield across the road. I walked over, stepped among the plants, and leaned down to be sure. It was the corn, growing.